DID JESUS REALLY RISE FROM THE DEAD?

"Dr. Miller has powerfully and uniquely described the resurrection of Jesus Christ, making it intellectually tenable to the scientific mind."

CARL E. HAISCH, Professor of Surgery, Director of Surgical Education, Associate Dean for Faculty Development, East Carolina University

"While many books have been written about the resurrection of Jesus Christ, both pro and con, this work is one-of-a-kind. Most references cite evidence using both medical and scientific expertise. As an accomplished practicing surgeon and research scientist, Miller has approached this book methodically and comprehensively after devoting many years of study. This is an outstanding resource for anyone questioning the authenticity of the resurrection, or for those seeking to better understand the foundation of the Christian faith."

JEANNIE FALWELL SAVAS, Associate Professor of Surgery, Virginia Commonwealth University; Chief of Surgery, McGuire Veterans Affairs Medical Center

"Miller has applied his knowledge of anatomy and physiology to bring the unspeakable reality of the crucifixion and death of Christ to our awareness as a prelude to applying the principles of scientific inquiry to a sound defense of the physical resurrection of Christ. The resurrection is pivotal to Miller's comprehensible, reflective, and personal apologetics of forgiveness, redemption, and restoration. Those seeking truth will be clearly directed to the Way. The wealth of physical and scriptural support for the crucified and resurrected Christ will reaffirm the believer's convictions."

GORDON L. KAUFFMAN, JR., MD, Steven and Sharon Baron Professor of Surgery, Professor of Physiology, Humanities and Medicine, The Penn State University College of Medicine

"It is a distinct pleasure for me to highly endorse this book. I worked with Dr. Miller for many years when he was Professor of Surgery at the University of Texas Medical School. His educational credentials strongly validate him as an excellent clinical surgeon and as an outstanding researcher in the basic science of medicine. Dr. Miller is uniquely qualified as a scientist to write about the resurrection of Jesus because he is thoroughly familiar with the scientific method, which he uses throughout his book. All scientific analyses are documented and footnoted, and resources for additional investigation are given. As an academic researcher, his conclusions are stated carefully and accurately based on the data. This book is a 'must read' for those who are searching for truth and a logical, unbiased evaluation of the facts concerning the physical resurrection of Jesus."

BRUCE V. MACFADYEN, Professor of Surgery, University of Texas Medical School Houston

DID JESUS REALLY RISE FROM THE DEAD?

A Surgeon-Scientist Examines the Evidence

THOMAS A. MILLER, MD

WHEATON, ILLINOIS

Did Jesus Really Rise from the Dead? A Surgeon-Scientist Examines the Evidence

Copyright © 2013 by Thomas A. Miller

Published by Crossway
    1300 Crescent Street
    Wheaton, Illinois 60187

Cover design and image: Joe Cavazos

First printing 2013

Printed in the United States of America

Trade paperback ISBN: 978-1-4335-3307-5
PDF ISBN: 978-1-4335-3308-2
Mobipocket ISBN: 978-1-4335-3309-9
ePub ISBN: 978-1-4335-3310-5

Library of Congress Cataloging-in-Publication Data

Miller, Thomas A. (Thomas Allen), 1944–
    p.   cm.
    Includes bibliographical references and index.
    ISBN 978-1-4335-3307-5 (tp)
    1. Jesus Christ—Resurrection. 2. Jesus Christ—Historicity. I. Title.
BT482.M55   2013
232.9'7—dc23   2012038138

Crossway is a publishing ministry of Good News Publishers.

VP   22   21   20   19   18   17   16   15   14   13
14   13   12   11   10   9   8   7   6   5   4   3   2   1

CONTENTS

ACKNOWLEDGMENTS

In writing any book, many people are involved along the way, assisting in its development and ultimate completion. A special thanks goes to Doris Farquhar, a friend and professional colleague, whom I have known for more than thirty years. An expert typist and computer person, she helped get each chapter formatted so that it met publication specifications. This was no small feat, since my type A personality was constantly asking her to redo things to get them perfect. Much gratitude, Doris, for what you did to make this book a reality. My thanks as well to my colleague and fellow surgeon Dr. Jeannie Savas, who reviewed the statistics in chapter 5 and offered comments to make it more compelling. Her mathematical and statistical background proved invaluable in helping me make my case. My appreciation, Jeannie, for your assistance and friendship.

Bringing this book to publication was a new kind of venture for me. All my previous publications were in the scientific arena, where I knew the "players" well and could pick up the phone and discuss ideas with them. Publishing in the Christian world was new to me and clearly uncharted territory. God was gracious, however, and enabled me to meet Dr. Robert Peterson, professor of systematic theology at Covenant Seminary in St. Louis, when he presented a weekend conference at our church. Almost immediately we "hit it off," and he showed a genuine interest in this project. Over the next year we talked on the phone and e-mailed each other many times. This communication helped greatly. Further, it was his doing that put me in touch with Crossway. Thank you, Robert, for this ministry of grace.

What an exciting day it was when I received an e-mail from Allan Fisher at Crossway, telling me that my proposal was positively received and that Crossway wanted to work with me. I am deeply grateful, Crossway, for giving me this opportunity. My special thanks to Jill

Carter, who has been my editorial contact at Crossway, and who has helped in so many ways. You have been such a delight to work with. Appreciation is also offered to Justin Taylor, who worked with me in "hammering out" an acceptable title for the book. Your patience and kindness did not go unnoticed. Enough cannot be said about Bill Deckard, who was given the monumental task of reading and editing the entire book. You truly are a master at making thoughts "smoothly flow" and bringing coherence to my arguments. My gratitude for a job well done!

Although all the people just named have been wonderful friends and colleagues, this book would not have been possible without the support of my family. A special thanks to my three children, Laurie, David (and his wife Laurel), and Bill (and his wife Emily), who encouraged me from the beginning. I love you all. An additional note of appreciation to Bill and Emily for the many hours they devoted to initially typing most of the chapters and helping to format them so that they were readable and made sense. My brother-in-law, Bob Walters, went the extra mile in typing the last chapter. Thank you, Bob, for such generosity. Finally, words are not adequate to express the feelings I have for my wife, Janet, and the support she gave while writing this book. Thanks for your love, encouragement, and continual belief in me over these past forty-four years. Marrying you has truly brought much joy and happiness. I love you!

I would like to clearly affirm that the beliefs and opinions stated in this book are solely my own, and should in no way be interpreted as representing the viewpoints of the academic and professional institutions with which I am associated.

Finally, any errors or misrepresentations that may be discovered in reading this book, while not intentional, are a product of my own human imperfections and should not be attributed to my publisher.

INTRODUCTION

The present book has been some twenty-plus years in the making. Much of the material has been the ongoing subject of a series of lectures given to various groups concerning the resurrection of Jesus Christ and why I believe it actually happened. When initially asked to make these presentations, the interest in my doing so derived from the fact that I was a surgeon and research scientist on the faculty of a major medical school who saw no conflict with also being a believer in Jesus Christ.

While my approach to these presentations was no different than it would have been for any other talk I might have given on some research or clinical topic—namely, evidence-based—I quickly learned that their appeal was precisely for that reason. People hearing these discussions would commonly tell me that the way the information was conveyed was much more compelling than what they usually heard articulated in a sermon or Sunday school class on this subject. In their minds, I was not satisfied with rehashing religious dogma but instead had a desire to probe deeper to see whether the biblical message really did resonate with what goes on in the "real" world. In one sense I was quite bothered that many of the things I was saying were apparently "new" to people who were regular church attendees and should have at least known the basics of the evidence for the resurrection of Christ. At the same time, I was gratified that God was seemingly using me to minister to individuals who had doubts or misgivings about the relevance and authenticity of the gospel, particularly the resurrection. Although it was never my plan to actually write a book on the resurrection, it has become increasingly apparent in recent years that a volume addressing this issue as seen through the eyes of a surgeon-scientist might prove helpful, especially for those who struggle with the validity of such a mind-boggling event as someone rising from the dead.

Despite the relativity and ambiguity that defines and characterizes much of the postmodern world in which we live in these opening days of the twenty-first century, I believe that truth still matters and that without it one is faced with a rudderless life, adrift and without purpose. But for truth to have any meaning, it must have an unshakeable foundation, and that foundation, to be believed, depends on evidence that is consistent and dependable. This is what makes science so appealing: it is evidence-based and refuses to accept something as true unless that evidence can stand up under the most rigorous scrutiny and analysis. Little wonder, then, that "faith" is often viewed as superstition, and anything having a religious flavor is considered myth, fantasy, or downright fraud. God, miracles, and especially something as strange as a resurrection evokes an attitude of "you've got to be kidding" for many in the scientific world, and outright disbelief in those who consider themselves part of the intellectual elite. But is truth only that which science says is true and which can be assessed scientifically? And are science and religion really incompatible?

This book was written to challenge these notions and to argue that if one is willing to be open-minded and objective, and to assess the evidence with fairness and on its own merits, a powerful case can be made for the resurrection of Jesus Christ as a verifiable historical event. Since there is no way to study a resurrection using the tools and methods commonly employed in science, how does one evaluate the possibility that Jesus really did rise from the dead? This is accomplished by keeping in mind that, as an alleged historical event that presumably took place some twenty centuries ago, it needs to be examined like any other historical event. This includes determining what happened when the event supposedly occurred, assessing the reliability of the eyewitnesses and the documents purporting to describe the event, and considering the historical consequences of the event that cannot be logically explained unless the event really did occur. It is precisely on the basis of the evidence obtained after analyzing these considerations that I contend that the historicity of the resurrection is as secure as any scientific finding that I have personally obtained or observed in the research laboratory. On this basis I contend that Christ's resurrection is the greatest event in human history, an event that should not and cannot be ignored.

While it is hoped that a diverse audience will benefit from this discussion of the resurrection, it is written especially for those who are dissatisfied with "pat answers." It is one thing to say you believe in the resurrection of Jesus Christ, but it is quite another to know why you believe, and what it means. If asked to defend this truth, what would you say? It is not good enough to simply respond, "I believe it because the Bible teaches it." In this age of disbelief and skepticism, people want compelling evidence. It has been regrettably obvious to me while giving my lectures over the past two decades that the contemporary church has failed in offering a vigorous and evidence-based defense of the resurrection and that this failure is a substantial reason why organized religion has been so ineffectual in reaching the unchurched. Perhaps you are among this group. In many pulpits, the resurrection is treated as an afterthought—and in some pulpits, not believed at all—rather than being acknowledged as the pivotal point on which Christianity stands or falls. As the apostle Paul so firmly stated (see 1 Cor. 15:17–19), if the resurrection did not occur, our faith is futile and we are still in our sins. It is my prayer, then, that this book can be used in some small way to help rectify this situation.

In the end, this book is the testimony of a surgeon-scientist who during his college years first came to believe that the resurrection of Jesus Christ really did occur. Over the subsequent forty-seven years, and despite being steeped in science and the challenges of a naturalistic worldview so prevalent in this discipline, he has continued to embrace that conviction. Why? Because the evidence supporting the resurrection is exceedingly compelling and can stand up under the toughest scrutiny. If you are willing to review that evidence and determine for yourself whether it can be trusted, this book was written with you in mind.

1

CAN A CREDIBLE SCIENTIST REALLY BELIEVE IN THE RESURRECTION?

I never intended to write a book on the resurrection. After all, isn't that a theological issue, and why would a person steeped in science all of his professional life write about something that is clearly outside of his field? And furthermore, we all know that if something can't be proved by science, it either can't be known or isn't worth knowing, including such things as God, the supernatural, and, of all absurdities, rising from the dead. Or might we be wrong, and might those religious types be right after all? What if a resurrection really did happen to a man named Jesus, as the Christian religion has claimed for nearly two thousand years? Wouldn't such an event be something worth knowing about? But I'm getting ahead of myself. Before dealing with these issues, you need to know something about me and how this all came about.

The Shaping of My Worldview

I grew up in a devoutly religious family with a strong Christian worldview. As such, I was exposed early on to the belief that the resurrection of Jesus had actually occurred and was not a figment of some theological imagination. The tenacity with which my parents embraced this belief rubbed off on me, and I too became a believer early in childhood. This belief was a borrowed one, however, and it was many years later before the reality of what the resurrection means became clear to me, not to mention the implications it would have on my own worldview. It was not until my undergraduate years at Wheaton College that I was exposed to any rigorous discussion of the resurrection. Wheaton is a small Christian liberal arts college in Wheaton, Illinois, about twenty-five miles west of Chicago. Founded in the middle of the nineteenth century, its motto is "For Christ and His Kingdom."[1] One might appropriately ask how I ended up at this school. Actually, it was quite logical. When a person is reared in the kind of family I was, a strong emphasis is placed on gaining one's education in a Christian environment. Hence, studying at a school like Wheaton would be quite consistent with that orientation.

Although Wheaton is sometimes maligned and accused of being anti-intellectual because of its religious underpinnings, my experience as a student at Wheaton was anything but that. I found the environment to be intellectually challenging, with an openness to a variety of thought processes, many in direct opposition to what Wheaton stood for foundationally. It is true that the Bible was taken seriously, but such commitment was never at the expense of free speech, open dialogue on controversial topics, or academic freedom. Although I was initially uncertain regarding which career path I would pursue, as most entering college students are, my early exposure to chemistry and biology quickly assured me that a career in medicine was the best fit. The premedical curriculum was excellent. While I majored in zoology and minored in chemistry, the liberal arts emphasis at Wheaton enabled me to take an abundance of courses in history, philosophy, and religion. It was the intellectual rigor with which these disciplines were taught that greatly impacted the Christian worldview that I ultimately embraced as my own. Further, an apologetics course[2] I took as a senior absolved any doubts I might have had regarding the historicity of the resurrection. Thus, I became absolutely convinced that Jesus did in fact rise from the dead.

My medical school training was obtained at Temple University in Philadelphia. It was during my Temple years that I met Janet, who

---

[1] Information about Wheaton College can be obtained from its website at www.wheaton.edu.
[2] Apologetics is the branch of theology focused on defending Christianity and its belief system.

became my wife and soul mate. We were married during Christmas vacation of my junior year. After acquiring an MD degree, I interned in surgery at the University of Chicago Hospitals, followed by a residency in surgery at the University of Michigan Hospitals. While at Michigan, I made the decision to pursue a career in academic surgery. This means I decided to forego the private practice of surgery and instead pursue my clinical responsibilities in the context of being a medical school faculty member. This would allow me to teach, pursue research, and use my surgical skills to train residents (i.e., trainees) who were desirous of becoming surgeons like myself. After formal training in surgery at Michigan, I did two additional years of specialized study in gastrointestinal (GI) research to better prepare for an academic career. Since my clinical interests involved the GI tract, such research training seemed logical. Thus, our family (Janet and I had three children by this time) moved from Ann Arbor to Texas. The first research year was undertaken at the University of Texas Medical Branch in Galveston and the second at the University of Texas Medical School in Houston, forty miles away. My reason for choosing these two institutions was that they were both powerhouses of GI research at the time. I have never been disappointed with the research training received at these institutions.

It has now been more than thirty-five years since this formal training was completed. During these three-plus decades, I have had the good fortune of pursuing a very satisfying career in surgery as a faculty member at three excellent medical schools. This has enabled me to be at the forefront of advances in my field, assist in the care of thousands of patients, and have an almost daily involvement in teaching medical students the principles of surgery as well as training hundreds of residents for careers in surgery. I have also experienced the pleasure and excitement of running a research laboratory that has been actively engaged for more than a quarter of a century in studying the mechanisms by which the lining of the stomach and other portions of the GI tract protect themselves from injury. Much of this research has been funded by the National Institutes of Health, and the findings have been shared with colleagues through publications in numerous scientific journals.

The Inevitability of Death and Possibility of Resurrection

As I reflect back on this experience as a surgeon-scientist, many thoughts obviously come to mind, but two observations in particular surface that are directly germane to the reason for writing this book. The first relates to my continuous belief in the resurrection of Jesus. One might think that, having been immersed in science for these many years, I would long since have gotten over this "superstition." In actuality, the more I have reviewed and re-reviewed the evidence for this event, the more convinced I have become that it is not some theological myth but really did occur in our space-time world some twenty centuries ago. But how can one who calls himself a credible scientist accept a notion that clearly resides in the realm of the miraculous? And we all know that science has long ago disproved the validity of miracles. Or has it?

Before discussing this issue further, a second observation that requires comment is what I would call the inevitability of death. The older I get, the more certain the reality of death becomes. Not only have I observed this enemy of humankind with consistent regularity in the hospital setting, but I have also encountered it with increasing frequency among friends and relatives. While you may feel indestructible and currently enjoy excellent health, be assured that death will ultimately lay its claim. As Euripides, the Greek playwright, said many centuries ago, "Death is the debt that all men must pay."[3]

At the risk of sounding morbid, people in the medical profession are really in the business of delaying death. This is especially true in patients with cancer and heart disease. While none of us can ultimately prevent it, we certainly use every means possible to forestall death, and in so doing we try to provide the best possible quality of life for our patients. We emphasize the importance of daily exercise and healthy eating and living so that disorders like diabetes, heart dis-

---

[3] Euripides was a Greek poet and playwright who lived from 480 to 406 BC. Some sources render his statement on death as, "But learn that to die is a debt we must all pay."

ease, obesity, and high blood pressure are minimized, with the goal of slowing the aging process—recognizing unfortunately that one's own mortality will eventually win out.

While all physicians deal with death on a somewhat regular basis, surgeons belong to that unique breed of health care providers who are confronted with it in an "up close and personal" way. In the many years I have practiced surgery, I have been challenged with this scourge perhaps in excess of a thousand times. In my younger years in practice, I frequently took "trauma call," and it would not be unusual to be in the operating room for many hours, sometimes all night, trying to put a patient back together who had been the victim of a serious motor vehicle accident or gunshot wound—just from being "in the wrong place at the wrong time." Although we saved many of these patients, many did not survive. Breaking the news to the family that their loved one had died was always difficult, especially when the patient was young.

Although I have not taken care of trauma victims in any regular way for the past fifteen years, I still have to deal with death much more frequently than I would prefer. Many of my patients have some form of cancer that, despite my best efforts, will eventually shorten their lives. I may be able to remove the cancer's primary focus or "debulk" its adverse effects on surrounding organs to improve the patient's quality of life, but if it has spread to other parts of the body, its lethal effects will ultimately win out. Similarly, I may be able to remove a diseased gall bladder, repair a groin hernia that has been causing pain, or lyse adhesions that have caused a bowel obstruction, but if the individual subjected to one of these procedures has a diseased heart, difficult to manage diabetes, or an elevated blood pressure that fails to respond to conventional medication, complications from one of these disorders may ultimately supersede whatever skill I may be able to offer in attending to their surgical problem. The net result is a compromised life span and sometimes a very unanticipated death.

While it is not uncommon for a patient to want to know something about my surgical abilities before giving their consent for the operation, the simple question of survival is much more common. No matter how routine the procedure, they almost always ask, "What are my chances of dying?" Why? Because no one wants to die. No matter how serious their disease may be, they want to be alive to enjoy life when the operation is completed. Though not often, some patients even refuse an operation if the chance of dying is more than they are willing to risk. Sometimes the pain that could be corrected by the operation becomes less of an issue if the risk of death is more than they had bargained for. What does this tell us about life itself? It tells us that life is precious, and that each of us wishes to live as long as possible even though we know that someday the "grim reaper" will pay us a visit. In short, no one wants to die.

So what does this have to do with a resurrection? Actually, everything. The fact that death is the great leveler and will ultimately lay claim on each of us, despite the impressive strides that have occurred in medicine and surgery during the past fifty years, makes the possibility of life beyond the grave not just some interesting topic for academic debate, but exceedingly relevant and important for every human being. It is in this context that a man named Jesus cannot be ignored. While most people acknowledge that he was a great religious teacher who lived in the early part of the first century, the claim that he overcame death and actually rose from the dead after being brutally murdered by crucifixion is the most important assertion in human history. If he merely died and remains entombed somewhere in the Middle East, he is no different from anyone else who has ever died. Simply put, he was a man and he died like a man. On the other hand, if the resurrection really happened, as the Christian religion has preached for some twenty centuries, that puts a whole different twist on this event and on the question of who Jesus was. For now one is forced to conclude that he was more than a mortal man—indeed, that he was actually a superman! This would further indicate that somehow he had power or access to power that was more than natural; in short, he was supernatural. This being so, the fact that he conquered death equally suggests that he could conceivably exercise that power for others, perhaps even for you and me, and that there really is such a thing as life after death. If this is true, such information has ramifications that affect the entire human race, and it therefore needs to be widely disseminated. What is particularly stunning is the bold statement that Jesus made in John's Gospel when raising his friend Lazarus from the dead. In no uncertain terms he declared, "I am the resurrection and the life. Whoever believes in me, though he die, yet shall he live, and everyone who lives and believes in me shall never die" (John 11:25–26). If this statement is really true, it means that not only did the man called Jesus conquer death for himself, but he conquered it also for you and me.

Scientific Truth versus Christian Belief

"But," you may say, "can anyone really believe this stuff in the twenty-first century?" Returning to the question that I left unanswered, "Can any respectable scientist really accept something as mind-boggling as a resurrection when we all know that miracles do not happen?" A considerable number in the scientific community would answer these questions with a resounding no. People like me who claim to be credible scientists but yet give credence to such a far-fetched idea as resurrection are clearly in the minority among our fellow scientists. After all, in this enlightened age, everyone knows that the "miraculous" simply does not occur. But is that really true? And on what basis? One need only go back to an earlier time in the history of science, when many of the great discoveries were made that have enabled present-day scientific advances, and a whole different mindset is evident.

Consider, for example, Isaac Newton, Johannes Kepler, Robert Boyle, and Michael Faraday. No one would dispute that these four men were some of the greatest scientists of all time. Newton's description of gravity and the laws of motion, Kepler's study of the planets and their rotational movements, Boyle's elucidation of the properties of gases, and Faraday's unraveling of the properties of electricity and electromagnetism clearly rank among the outstanding accomplishments in the history of science.[4] What is often forgotten is that each

---

[4]For information on these four scientists, see: Charles E. Hummel, *Galileo Connection: Resolving Conflicts between Science and the Bible* (Downers Grove, IL: InterVarsity Press, 1986), 61–62, 73–74, and 76–79, regarding Johannes Kepler; David L. Woodall, "The Relationship between Science and Scripture in the Thought of Robert Boyle," *Perspectives on Science and Christian Faith* 49 (1997): 32–39 (published by American Scientific Affiliation); Phillip Eichman, "The Christian Character of

of these men was a serious Christian and had no difficulty believing in the resurrection of Jesus, despite being a credible scientist. In fact, Newton wrote more about his religious beliefs than about his scientific observations![5] One might argue that had these individuals lived in our time, their religious persuasions would likely have been less important or would have been undermined entirely as they became aware of the ability of science to disprove things previously taken for granted. Obviously, the impact of modernity on their beliefs will never be known, but, perusing their writings, one quickly senses that these scientists did not believe that science was the be-all and end-all" that many scientists in our contemporary world think that it is. These earlier scientists understood that much of reality simply cannot be adequately explained using scientific methodology alone. For them, the universe and all of its wonder was the glorious expression of a magnificent God, and to study it was not only a high privilege and honor but a means of worshiping God's majesty. Thus, God's spontaneous and unpredictable intervention at times in the form of what we would call a miracle—the resurrection being the prime example—would in no way be in conflict with the usual orderliness of the universe and its laws, with which those four men were intimately acquainted.

This attitude of an earlier time is in marked contrast with what we observe today. Why? Because many modern scientists are so convinced of the ability of science to answer questions that, if something cannot be validated using scientific methods, it is viewed as either being unknowable or not existing at all. Perhaps the most visible example of this mentality presently is the evolutionary biologist and geneticist Richard Dawkins. In his book *The God Delusion*, Dawkins makes it abundantly clear that, for him, scientific truth is the only truth, and anything not provable by science is unknowable. Anything that even hints of being outside a scientific explanation is laughable at

Michael Faraday as Revealed in His Personal Life and Recorded Sermons," *Perspectives on Science and Christian Faith* 43 (1991): 92–95; Mitch Stokes, *Isaac Newton: Christian Encounter Series* (Nashville: Thomas Nelson, 2010).
[5] On Newton's religious writings, see Brad Harrub, "Isaac Newton—Religious Works Finally Published," at www.ApologeticsPress—Isaac Newton—Religious Works.

best and intellectually absurd at worst.[6] Using such logic (some would call it presupposition), he debunks any notion of the existence of God. He blatantly disregards any evidence that cannot be tested and verified using the tools of science, and because God is in such a category, for Dawkins he almost certainly is a delusion. Dawkins totally dismisses the idea of resurrection as academic rubbish, since to believe in such an event would require believing in a miracle, and obviously any legitimate scientist knows that miracles simply don't occur. For those who would even attempt to challenge this stance, Dawkins conveniently bypasses any serious discussion of evidence for a resurrection by insisting that modern scholarship has clearly shown that the New Testament Gospels (which are the primary sources describing the resurrection) are not reliable historical accounts about Jesus, since they were written long after his alleged death by individuals who clearly did not know him, making the possibility of myth and legend very likely. Dawkins derives many of these conclusions from a few selected sources that are clearly on the fringe and at odds with the thinking of most modern-day scholars. Notably absent is any discussion of the preponderance of contemporary New Testament scholarship, which offers an entirely different analysis of the Gospels. Not only does this scholarship challenge much of what is presented as the "final" word in Dawkins's book, but it also provides overwhelming evidence that the Gospels are very reliable historical sources, that they were written much earlier than originally thought, and that their writers either knew Jesus personally or were acquainted with those who did know him (more about this in the next chapter).

Unfortunately, the Dawkins mentality is not unique and is becoming much more commonplace in contemporary science. What is troubling about this type of thinking is that it has elevated science to a level of superiority that supersedes all other means of truth acquisition. As a result of its incredible success in advancing knowledge, especially within the last several decades, there has been a regrettable tendency among a growing number of scientists to claim that science is so powerful in its

---

[6] Richard Dawkins, *The God Delusion* (New York: Houghton Mifflin, 2006).

ability to explain things that in the not-too-distant future it will be able to provide an explanation for all phenomena. In many scientific circles, the only evidence worth considering when evaluating the truthfulness of something is that which can be assessed scientifically.

In responding to Dawkins and others who espouse this view, British theologian Alister McGrath (who also has a doctorate from Oxford in molecular biophysics), along with his wife, Joanna Collicutt McGrath (who likewise is trained in both theology and science [neuropsychology]), have this to say in their book *The Dawkins Delusion?*:

> . . . let's be quite clear that suggesting that science may have its limits is in no way a criticism or defamation of the scientific method. Dawkins does, I have to say with regret, tend to portray anyone raising questions about the scope of the sciences as a science-hating idiot. Yet there is a genuine question here. Every intellectual tool that we possess needs to be calibrated—in other words, to be examined to identify the conditions under which it is reliable. The question of whether science has limits is certainly not improper, nor does a positive answer to the question in any way represent a lapse into some kind of superstition. It is simply a legitimate demand for calibration of intellectual accuracy.[7]

In dealing with questions of meaning and purpose, the McGraths offer these additional insights:

> . . . there are many questions that by their very nature must be recognized to lie beyond the legitimate scope of scientific method, as this is normally understood. For example, is there a purpose within nature? Dawkins regards this as a spurious non-question. Yet this is hardly an illegitimate question for human beings to ask or to hope to have answered . . . . The question cannot be dismissed as illegitimate or nonsensical; it is simply being declared to lie beyond the scope of the scientific method. If it can be answered, it must be answered on other grounds.[8]

Accordingly, it must be emphasized that science deals with observation, with things that can be measured, analyzed, and quantified. Much in our lives falls outside the realm of those capabilities. For

---

[7] Alister McGrath and Joanna Collicutt McGrath, *The Dawkins Delusion? Atheist Fundamentalism and the Denial of the Divine* (Downers Grove, IL: InterVarsity Press, 2007), 36.
[8] Ibid., 38.

example, how does one analyze or quantify love, mercy, forgiveness, or hope? And yet these acts or needs are very common components of our everyday lives. One may be very much in love and may know beyond any doubt that the experience is real, but there is no way to validate or evaluate this scientifically. Further, one may be forgiven by another for a transgression that took place, but there is no way to quantify this forgiveness and how genuine it was using scientific methodology. Similarly, how do we know there is not an unseen world out there even though it does not lend itself to scientific analysis? And what about miracles? Or even God? Science cannot and never will be able to answer such questions, because the means by which it evaluates things and derives truth was never intended to do so. This does not mean that these questions are not worth attempting to answer but simply that science is not capable of providing any useful information regarding them. To be sure, science has unraveled a host of incredible mysteries in our universe, but it is simply incapable of unraveling the things just enumerated that concern us so deeply in our everyday lives.

One must be very careful in dismissing evidence that supports such realities simply because it cannot be subjected to scientific analysis. Evidence should always be assessed on its own merits. Evidence should inform one's view, rather than being dismissed as impossible simply on the basis of presuppositions. As objective as we humans like to think we are, virtually every one of us is vulnerable to the temptation of holding onto our "pet beliefs" even in the face of iron-clad evidence to the contrary.

In dealing with evidence, we sometimes get sidetracked by the possible implications of that evidence, so that we are hesitant to move forward in adequately evaluating the evidence itself. If the implications of accepting a certain piece of evidence challenge what we believe or are willing to believe, we dismiss the evidence as irrelevant and fail to consider it further. But ignoring evidence because we don't like its implications does not automatically invalidate the evidence. After careful assessment, the evidence may indeed turn out to be invalid, but the fear of possible implication should never be a criterion for the careful and objective analysis of evidence. Evidence for the resurrection is a prime example. To refuse to deal with the evidence allegedly supporting the resurrection simply because we believe a priori that the supernatural does not exist is not only intellectually dishonest; it suggests a certain arrogance, implying that we already know the truth despite what the evidence may indicate otherwise.

Unfortunately, when presented with an issue such as the resurrection of a person from the dead, there tends to be an emotional recoiling effect on the part of those who have no tolerance for an event that cannot be explained in naturalistic terms, and immediately a barrier of resistance is set up that restricts any further discussion. Such opposition is often encountered in the contemporary scientific community. For the hard-core scientist who has no room in his worldview for anything that cannot be rationally explained in naturalistic terms, to even consider something as outlandish as a resurrection (which evokes the possibility of the supernatural) deserves no further discussion, no matter how convincing the evidence may be. Resurrections simply do not happen! Once a person dies, he is dead, never to be alive again. Case closed!

Lest one think I am stretching the point, it is appropriate to reference Dawkins again. He considers a resurrection to be in the same category as a fairy tale like "Jack and the Beanstalk," and relegates anyone believing in such an event as clearly being irrational.[9] Notwithstanding such insults, it is noteworthy that nowhere in *The God Delusion* does he discuss the evidence for the resurrection, let alone evaluate the merits of this evidence. He simply has declared that it could not possibly have happened. Of equal note are the comments of William B. Provine, professor of biological sciences at Cornell University, regarding end of life issues:

> Let me summarize my views on what modern evolutionary biology tells us loud and clear. . . . There are no gods, no purposes, no goal-directed forces of any kind. There is no life after death. When I die, I am absolutely certain that I am going to be dead. That's the end for me.[10]

[9] Richard Dawkins, "You Ask the Questions Special," *The Independent*, December 4, 2006.
[10] William B. Provine, in "Darwinism: Science or Naturalistic Philosophy" (debate between William B. Provine and Phillip E. Johnson at Stanford University, April 30, 1994; published in *Origins Research* 16/1 [Fall/Winter 1994]: 9). Used by permission of Access Research Network, www.arn.org.

While Dawkins and Provine are certainly entitled to their opinions, there is nothing inherent in being an evolutionary biologist that is inconsistent with or in conflict with belief in God, life after death, or resurrection from the dead, despite what they might say and espouse. Several of my scientific friends are strong proponents of Darwinian evolution and at the same time possess an equally strong belief in God and the resurrection of Jesus. In fact, the current director of the National Institutes of Health and previous director of the National Human Genome Project, Francis Collins, MD, Ph.D., has written about his theistic outlook on life and belief in the resurrection in the book *The Language of God,* while at the same time endorsing evolutionary biology.[11] Considered by many to be the greatest geneticist of the present era, Collins sees no conflict between his credibility as a scientist and his Christian worldview.

Equally noteworthy is the observation that a considerable number of Nobel laureates have gone on record and indicated that they see no conflict between science and the supernatural and find the two worlds of inquiry complementary rather than contradictory—similar to the views of Newton, Kepler, Boyle, and Faraday in earlier times. Several more recent laureates, including Sir John Eccles (1963 in medicine), Charles Townes (1964 in physics), Joseph E. Murray (1990 in medicine), Richard Smalley (1996 in chemistry), and William D. Phillips (1997 in physics) have stated in writing their strong belief in God and the supernatural and have not been ashamed to call themselves Christians with all that such a designation means.[12]

One scientist who has been particularly vocal regarding his Christian faith and belief in the resurrection is the late esteemed astronomer Allan Sandage. Trained by Edwin Hubble (of Hubble telescope

---

[11] Francis S. Collins, *The Language of God: A Scientist Presents Evidence for Belief* (New York: Free Press, 2006).

[12] In *The God Delusion,* Dawkins stated that he could find only six scientific Nobel laureates who claimed to be Christians, when researched under the website heading "Nobel Prize-winning Scientific Christians." When he researched this further, four of these six were not Nobel-prize winners at all (see page 126 of his book). In contrast, in addition to the five Nobel laureates in science I have listed, there are also at least twenty-two others that I have found who have expressed a strong faith in God, the large majority also indicating that they were Christians and saw no conflict with being a Christian and also being a serious scientist. See Tihomir Dimitrov, "50 Nobel Laureates and Other Great Scientists Who Believe in God," *Scientific GOD Journal* 1/3 (March 2010): 143–273 (www.SciGOD.com).

fame) and moving forward with Hubble's research program following his untimely death in 1953, Sandage is known the world over for his important contributions concerning the size, age, shape, and fate of the cosmos. Such achievements earned him the prestigious Crafoord Prize, which is the Royal Swedish Academy's equivalent of the Nobel Prize for astronomy. Examining the evidence for Christianity in his later adulthood because of disenchantment with his avowed atheism, Sandage eventually converted and became a strong advocate of the Christian worldview. When questioned about the all too common presumption that there must necessarily be a conflict between science and religion, he offered these thoughts:

> Science makes explicit the quite incredible natural order, the interconnections at many levels between the laws of physics, the chemical reactions in the biological processes of life, etc. But science can answer only a fixed type of question. It is concerned with the *what, when,* and *how.* It does not, and indeed cannot, answer within its method (powerful as that method is), *why.*
>
> Why is there something instead of nothing? Why do all electrons have the same charge and mass? Why is the design that we see everywhere so truly miraculous? Why are so many processes so deeply interconnected?
>
> But we must admit that those scientists that *want* to see design *will* see design. Those that are content in every part of their being to live as materialistic reductionalists (*as we must all do as scientists in the laboratory, which is the place of the practice of our craft*) will never admit to a mystery of the design they see, always putting off by one step at a time, awaiting a reductionalist explanation for the present unknown. But to take this reductionalist belief to the deepest level and to an indefinite time into the future (and it will always remain indefinite) when "science will know everything" is itself an act of faith which denies that there can be anything unknown to science, even in principle. But things of the spirit are not things of science.
>
> There need be no conflict between science and religion if each appreciates its own boundaries and if each takes seriously the claims of the other. The proven success of science simply cannot be ignored by the church. But neither can the church's claim to explain the world at the very deepest level be dismissed. If God did not exist, science would have to (and indeed has) invent the concept to explain what it is discovering at its core. . . .
>
> If there is no God, nothing makes sense. The atheist's case is based on a deception they wish to play upon themselves that follows already

from their initial premise. And if there *is* a God, he must be true both to science and religion. If it seems not so, then one's hermeneutics (either the pastor's or the scientist's) must [be] wrong.[13]

So is Dawkins right that anyone who calls himself or herself a serious scientist cannot possibly believe in God or possess a religious faith? Based on the foregoing considerations, clearly not. Further, a fitting rebuttal to Dawkins's arguments are the words of the late Harvard biologist Stephen Jay Gould, when commenting on the religious faith of many of his friends and colleagues who were also scientists. Even though he considered himself an atheist, he had this to say:

> Either half of my colleagues are enormously stupid, or else the science of Darwinism is fully compatible with conventional religious beliefs—and equally compatible with atheism.[14]

It should be obvious from the preceding discussion that a person can be a respected scientist, and even achieve celebrated status, and at the same time believe in God and possess a vibrant Christian faith that also encompasses belief in Jesus's resurrection. What may be surprising is that this circumstance is more common than one might have thought. Hundreds, if not thousands, of contemporary scientists have stated, without apology, their conviction that the relationship between science and religion does not have to be an adversarial one, but can be one of compatibility and meaningful interaction allowing the free expression of religious faith as well as serious scientific endeavor.[15] Contrary to the notion of some, it is not necessary to leave one's "brain" on the doorsteps of a church prior to entering it for worship.

---

[13] Allan Sandage, "A Scientist Reflects on Religious Belief," 2; http://www.leaderu.com/truth/1truth15.html (used with permission); Sandage's conversion to Christianity is an interesting case study of a scientist coming to faith: see William A. Durbin, "Negotiating the Boundaries of Science and Religion: The Conversion of Allan Sandage" (www.alban.org/research.aspx?id=6394).

[14] Stephen Jay Gould, "Impeaching a Self-Appointed Judge," *Scientific American* 267/1 (1992): 118–121.

[15] Numerous resources are available detailing the substantial number of contemporary scientists who embrace the Christian faith. An extensive compilation of this information has been put together by W. R. Miller, "Scientists of the Christian Faith: A Presentation of the Pioneers, Practitioners, and Supporters of Modern Science" (www.tektonics.org/scim/sciencemony.htm); in addition, the American Scientific Affiliation was organized in the 1940s and continues to investigate issues relating to Christian faith and science from an evangelical perspective; its membership extends into the thousands (http//www.asa3.org/).

"But I'm not convinced," I hear someone say. "It's perfectly fine if other scientists want to embrace religion and see no conflict between science and religious faith, but as for me, I still have huge problems with the issue of miracles, and especially something as bizarre as a resurrection. It seems to me that science has pretty much disproved the possibility of miracles! After all, if the laws of nature are inviolate and immutable, as they seem to be, how can miracles occur, since they would obviously have to alter those laws, and we know that simply doesn't happen?" While many in the scientific world embrace the notion that the laws of nature are fixed and necessarily true and thereby cannot change, it must be emphasized that what we call "laws" are in actuality human *descriptions* of what has been observed to occur and not fixed *prescriptions* of what must occur and invariably does occur with no possible exception. There is no question that such laws indeed tell us what can be anticipated to happen, and what does consistently happen under a given set of conditions, but there is no way that we can conclude, with *absolute 100 percent certainty*, that there will never be any interruptions. To offer such an assurance would require that we have complete knowledge of every nuance of what these laws are and how they have worked in the past, how they work in the present, and how they will work in the future under any and all circumstances by which they have been defined. Such verification is simply not achievable. Thus, there is always the possibility, albeit exceedingly rare, but nonetheless possible, no matter how hardwired our universe may be, that a law(s) of nature could be temporarily or momentarily superseded or modified without disrupting the overall function and stability of the world in which we live. Although a scientist observing such an unanticipated event may have no adequate explanation for its occurrence other than to call it an "anomaly"—since there is no way to study it because of its rarity and unpredictability—the possibility of divine causation must also be considered. In the latter circumstance, such an interruption could be a reflection of a Creator God interacting with his universe as he deems appropriate. In this situation, it would be called a supernatural intervention, or what is commonly referred to as miracle. Regardless of the explanation offered, science itself has no way of claiming which option is correct. If a scientist boldly declares that miracles are impossible, that assertion is a personal opinion reflecting his or her worldview, and nothing more.

Scientific Knowing versus Historical Knowing

So what do we conclude about the issue of Jesus's resurrection, since it would qualify as an unanticipated interruption of the laws of nature about death and its finality, and since it is apparent that there is no way to study this event scientifically? Have we exhausted our options in determining whether the resurrection really occurred, or is there some other way to unravel the truth regarding its validity?

When delivering the 2007 Gregory Lecture on the subject "Can a Scientist Believe in the Resurrection?" noted New Testament historian N. T. Wright emphasized the difference between "scientific knowing" and "historical knowing."[16] The former relies on repeatable events and makes decisions on the basis of that repeatability, whereas the latter is limited to assessing a onetime event that will never again happen in precisely the same way. Clearly, because of this lack of repeatability, the "scientific method" is severely limited in its ability to accurately assess historical issues. This by no means implies that a historical event cannot be validated as having occurred, but simply that the "tools of science" were not designed to render that validation.

The resurrection is such an event. If looked at through "the eyes of science" it is easy to conclude that it never occurred. But if evaluated as a historical event as one would evaluate any other possible historical event, and with the same objectivity and fairness, the conclusion that it could not have occurred may not be all that certain. It is in this context that the thoughts of N. T. Wright are especially applicable:

> To put it crudely, and again without all the necessary footnotes and nuances, science studies the repeatable, while history studies the unrepeatable. Caesar only crossed the Rubicon once, and if he'd crossed it again it would have meant something different the second time. There was, and could be, only one first landing on the moon. The fall

---

[16] N. T. Wright, "Can a Scientist Believe in the Resurrection?" (James Gregory Lecture, University of St. Andrews, 2007), www.philosophy-religion.org/world/pdfs/Tom-Wright-Lecturepdf.

of the second Jerusalem Temple took place in AD 70 and never happened again. Historians don't of course see this as a problem, and are usually not shy about declaring that these events certainly took place even though we can't repeat them in the laboratory. But when people say "but that can't have happened, because we know that *that sort of thing* does not actually happen," they are appealing to a kind of would-be scientific principle of history, namely the principle of *analogy*. The problem with analogy is that it never quite gets you far enough, precisely because history is full of unlikely things that happened once and once only, so that the analogies are often at best partial, and are dependent anyway on the retort "who says?" to the objection about some kinds of things not normally happening. And indeed, in the case in point, we should note as an obvious but often overlooked point the fact that the early Christians did *not* think that Jesus' resurrection was one instance of something that happened from time to time elsewhere. Granted, they saw it as the first, advance instance of something that would eventually happen to everyone else, but they didn't employ that future hope as an analogy from which to argue back that it had happened already in this one instance.

So how does the historian work when the evidence points towards things which we do not normally expect? The resurrection is such a prime example of this that it's hard to produce, at this meta-level, analogies for the question. But, sooner or later, questions of worldview begin to loom up in the background, and the question of what kinds of material the historian will allow on stage is inevitably affected by the worldview within which he or she lives. And at that point we are back to the question of the scientist who, faced with the thoroughly repeatable experiment of what happens to dead bodies, what has always, it seems, happened and what seems likely always to go on happening, declares that the evidence is so massive that it is impossible to believe in the resurrection without ceasing to be a scientist altogether.

This is the point at which we must switch tracks and go to the evidence itself. What can be said, within whatever can be called scientific historiography, about the proposition that Jesus of Nazareth was bodily raised from the dead?"[17]

This challenge by Wright to "go to the evidence itself" leaves us with only two options. One is simply to decline any serious analysis of whatever evidential material may exist and dismiss it as being irrele-

---

[17] Ibid., 3 (I am grateful to N.T. Wright for permission to use this quote).

vant on the contention that dead people, even Jesus, simply do not rise from the dead. As a scientist, I would certainly be justified in choosing this option and would likely be applauded by many of my colleagues for making this choice and not wasting time in such a pursuit. In the end, however, such resistance proves nothing. For if Jesus really did come back to life after dying, any denial by me or anyone else in no way nullifies that fact. Rather, this attitude simply indicates that the one taking such a stance possesses a certain level of stubbornness, some would say arrogance, in how he approaches the acquisition of truth, and that he may not be as unbiased and objective as he would like people to think he is. The other option is to take a hard, honest look at the evidence and determine if it can sustain rigorous scrutiny. It is precisely with that goal in mind that this book has been written.

I said earlier that I first became convinced that the resurrection was really true when I was confronted with the evidence for this event as an undergraduate student at Wheaton College. To say that this initial conviction settled the issue once and for all and that I never had any further doubts would be blatantly misleading. In fact, as my career unfolded and I became increasingly steeped in science, doubts began to surface that maybe the resurrection really was a hoax and that the evidence for this event was not as solid as I had originally thought. Could it be that my naivete as a college student made me accept something that simply was not as certain as I had thought, and that there were alternative explanations to account for the so-called evidence? However, each time I reassessed the evidence as doubts arose, I reached the same conclusion. Despite how astounding it might have appeared, I became repeatedly more convinced that Jesus really did conquer death! It has now been some forty-seven years since I sat in that college classroom, and I am more certain than ever that the resurrection is a historical fact.

What Is a Resurrection?

It is obvious if you are reading this chapter that you have more than just a casual interest in the resurrection. There are countless reasons why that might be, and only you know the specific one that has linked you with this book. Regardless of your reason, however, I think it is safe to say that at some level you want to know whether this event actually took place, and if so, what does it mean? As one who has taken this journey of inquiry, I want to make it crystal clear that if the resurrection of Jesus actually did take place, it is more than just another historical event. It is one thing to believe, on the basis of historical findings, that George Washington was the first president of the United States. That clearly was an important event in the history of our country and was crucial in determining what it would ultimately become. But as important as that event was, it pales by comparison with an event that involves a person coming back to life after clearly being dead. In fact, I would go so far as to contend that this event supersedes any other event that has ever taken place in human history and conjures up a whole litany of issues that now seem possible, such as the existence of a supernatural realm of reality, the existence of God, miracles, and even life after death.

But how credible is the evidence for that alleged event? Obviously I think it is quite credible or I would not have written this book. It is up to you to decide whether you agree. But before proceeding to examine the historicity of the resurrection, a clear definition of "resurrection" is absolutely essential. When it is stated that Jesus rose from the dead, what precisely are we talking about? Although some have used the word *resuscitation* as a synonym for resurrection, a resuscitation is not a resurrection. Resurrection implies that a person who was truly dead has come back to life. Resuscitation, on the other hand, is a circumstance where life-sustaining substances are temporarily unavailable to the body, but if quickly and adequately re-provided organ death (and the death of the cells making up that organ) will not occur. Resuscitation assumes that death has not yet occurred and that it can be prevented from occurring. The classic example of this circumstance in humans is cardiac arrest. When this happens, blood no longer flows through the body, depriving it of essential nutrients and oxygen. If the heart can be restarted and blood flow reestablished, we say that the patient has been resuscitated. Death never actually occurred, even though it could have if the resuscitation had not been successful.

A resurrection is also not a *revivification*. This latter word comes from the verb form "to revive." Again, when used in the context of a human body, it assumes that death has not occurred but that the body in question requires specialized care to help its organs (and the cells responsible for them) perform more efficiently, until such care is no longer needed. Patients requiring the expertise of intensive care in a hospital setting would be an example of revivification. When their ailing organs have regained new energy and efficiency from such care, it is not uncommon to say that they have been revived or "brought back from the dead" even though they never actually died. Another example would be the frozen storage of female egg cells or male sperm cells for couples having reproductive problems. These cells can be frozen for a considerable time with their life processes "temporarily suspended" in this frozen state, but such cells have not actually died. We know this because when the freezing is discontinued, the suspended life processes can be "revived." Otherwise, they would have no life-giving capabilities and would prove useless in producing babies for infertile couples.

Finally, a resurrection is not a *reincarnation*. Since this circumstance assumes that the previously occupied body has died, those who believe in reincarnation say that the soul/spirit from that body now is reincarnated into another body, most commonly an animal's body, sometimes a plant, and on occasion another human body. The resurrected Jesus, the New Testament Gospels assert, came back to life in a body fully recognizable as the "same body" he possessed before he died. Further, the fact that his crucified body truly died (see chapter 3) and remained dead until three days later eliminates any possibility of a resuscitation or revivification. Thus, when we talk about Jesus coming back to life after having died, we are defining a situation in which the body he possessed prior to death, and which was clearly dead when placed in the tomb, was reenergized with new life from its dead state so that materially and physically he was the same Jesus, and not some apparition or ghost. As preposterous as this may seem, the events surrounding Jesus's resurrection and the impact those events had on his disciples' lives, as we shall see, make no sense unless this physicality truly existed.

2

CAN THE NEW TESTAMENT (AND ESPECIALLY THE GOSPELS) BE TRUSTED?

Documentation is extremely important in the world of science. When a scientist performs an experiment in the laboratory or conducts a study involving human subjects, he does so with the intention of evaluating a certain problem that he considers important, and about which he wants to have a much better understanding. Assuming this goal is achieved, the findings are evaluated, conclusions are reached, and the results are documented in written form that usually ends up being published in some scientific journal. This written documentation serves at least three important purposes. First, the scientist doing the reporting is attesting to the reliability of the findings and, in his judgment, what they mean. Second, by affixing his name to the report he is personally verifying the integrity of the results and stating in writing that they were honestly obtained. Third, this written attestation provides an element of permanence for the research being reported so that future scientists have a historical record of what has been done, which they can use to help interpret their own findings. Without such documentation, one would have no knowledge of previous research in a particular scientific field. If our hypothetical scientist is unwilling to document his findings in written form, no matter how much or how enthusiastically he discusses them verbally, one can seriously question their credibility. Writing things down for others to read, and especially having them published, carries with it personal ownership.

In a similar way, documentation is absolutely crucial in any discussion of the resurrection of Jesus. It is one thing for some church body or religious organization to claim that Jesus rose from the dead, and even to have some long-standing tradition or creed attesting to that belief, but without some written verification that can be studied and analyzed, those of us living some twenty centuries after the alleged event have no way to determine its historicity. Thus, any discussion of a possible resurrection is meaningless without such documentary evidence.

Fortunately, we are not lacking in this evidentiary support. Not only is the biblical New Testament centered around the person of Jesus, but its first four books, the Gospels of Mathew, Mark, Luke, and John, are the major source material detailing his life, death, and resurrection. Although nonbiblical sources exist indicating that an individual named Jesus actually lived and is historically verifiable independent of the Gospels, none of these accounts provide any comprehensive information, and they are generally limited to a few paragraphs, rather than any substantive discussion of Jesus's earthly existence.[1] This being so, anyone interested in detailed information about Jesus is dependent on the reliability of these four Gospels. This issue becomes especially important if we are to reach any meaningful conclusions about the resurrection. So, how trustworthy are these biblical accounts? Actually, if one is willing to approach the material in the New Testament, and especially the Gospels, with the same fairness and openness that is granted other ancient documents, we find that the Gospels are exceedingly reliable. The "if" clause in that last sentence is particularly important, because there is a tendency among some scholars to hold the New Testament writings to a different standard than other ancient writings.

Evidence for New Testament Reliability

There are at least *four* lines of evidence that support the reliability of the New Testament Gospels as valid witnesses to the life and times

---

[1] Excellent source material regarding information about Jesus outside the Gospel accounts includes: Gary Habermas, *The Historical Jesus* (Joplin, MO: College Press, 1996), see especially chapter 9; Edwin Yamauchi, "Jesus Outside the New Testament: What Is the Evidence?" in *Jesus Under Fire*, ed. Michael Wilkins and J. P. Moreland (Grand Rapids, MI: Zondervan, 1995).

of Jesus. The first is what could be called the *manuscript proximity factor.*[2] To understand what this means, it must be remembered that there are *no* original manuscripts in existence for *any* writings detailing events that occurred in ancient times, whether they involve events recorded in the New Testament or those reported in other ancient writings. Since the printing press was not invented until the fifteenth century, we are totally dependent on hand-copied manuscripts for any information regarding ancient history. The accuracy of these manuscripts is greatly influenced by the integrity of the copyist (i.e., scribe) and how close the details of the copied manuscript are to the actual event being written about.

As an example of these considerations, suppose that a person living in the first century wrote an account of the destruction of Jerusalem by the Romans in AD 70. Let's further suppose that this person's original manuscript was copied by scribes, so that several dozen more copies, which we'll call first-generation copies, were available for dissemination. After this person's death, the original manuscript of his work was destroyed, as were most of the copies. During the second and third centuries, additional copies of this treatise were made by copying the text of the first-generation copies still available from the first century. These second-generation copies were then copied by other copyists to further distribute this work. These resultant third-generation copies were copied again, and those in turn another time, and so on and so on. Let's further suppose that, by the sixth century AD, all previous copies of this work had been destroyed and the only one available was in its seventh generation of copying. How reliable would this only extant copy of the original manuscript be? This would depend on how meticulous the copier of this remaining copy had been in copying the previous copy, and how compulsive each preceding copier had been in copying the one before it. If care and precision had prevailed with each subsequent copy, then the sixth-century copy would in all probability be an accurate and reliable representation of the original work. If not, the trustworthiness of the

---

[2] Josh McDowell, *Evidence for Christianity: Historical Evidence for the Christian Faith* (Nashville: Thomas Nelson, 2006), 60–66.

sixth-century copy could be called into question. Obviously, the less copying that occurs from the original manuscript, the more accurate a later copy is likely to be, assuming of course that each copyist involved was reliable as a copier and did not have some hidden agenda, such as adding or deleting material.

With these copying issues in mind, and recognizing that early manuscripts and copies of almost all ancient documents unfortunately have been destroyed, it should come as no surprise that the proximity of an available treatise or manuscript describing a particular ancient historical event varies widely with respect to the event being evaluated.[3] Homer's *Iliad* is a case in point. The earliest manuscript available is 400 years removed from when the work was actually written. Even more dramatic is the earliest copy of *The Gallic Wars* by Julius Caesar, which is separated by a thousand years from when it was originally written. Interestingly, the earliest manuscript evidence detailing

TABLE 2.1: Manuscript Proximity of Ancient Documents

AUTHOR	BOOK	DATE WRITTEN	EARLIEST COPIES	TIME GAP	NO. OF COPIES
Homer	*Iliad*	800 BC	c. 400 BC	c. 400 yrs.	643
Herodotus	*History*	480–425 BC	c. AD 900	c. 1,350 yrs.	8
Thucydides	*History*	460–400 BC	c. AD 900	c. 1,300 yrs.	8
Plato		400 BC	c. AD 900	c. 1,300 yrs.	7
Demosthenes		300 BC	c. AD 1100	c. 1,400 yrs.	200
Caesar	*Gallic Wars*	100–44 BC	c. AD 900	c. 1,000 yrs.	10
Livy	*History of Rome*	59 BC–AD 17	4th century (partial) mostly 10th century	c. 400 yrs. c. 1,000 yrs.	1 partial 19 copies
Tacitus	*Annals*	AD 100	c. AD 1100	c. 1,000 yrs.	20
Pliny Secundus	*Natural History*	AD 61–113	c. AD 850	c. 750 yrs.	7
New Testament		AD 50–100	c. 114 (fragment) c. 200 (books) c. 250 (most of N.T.) c. 325 (complete N.T.)	+50 yrs. 100 yrs. 150 yrs. 225 yrs.	5,366

Taken from: Josh McDowell, *Evidence for Christianity* (Nashville: Thomas Nelson, 2006), 65. (Used by permission of Thomas Nelson.) AUTHOR'S NOTE: The actual number of New Testament copies (in Greek) approaches 5,700; see table 2.2.

---

[3] Ibid.

events from the New Testament Gospels ranges from no more than 50 years (a fragment of John's Gospel) to about 225 years (complete manuscripts of the Gospels) from when the Gospels were originally written. Thus, when compared with the other ancient writings (see table 2.1), the Gospels have a far greater chance of being reliable than descriptions of various historical events from the ancient world that we usually take for granted.

Similar evidence supporting the validity of the Gospels is derived from the *manuscript number factor*.[4] The more manuscripts available detailing a particular time or event, the more likely the information can be trusted, especially if there are only minor differences among the copies. For example, if the hypothetical text referred to previously describing the downfall of Jerusalem in AD 70 had copies from the thirteenth century that were not appreciably different from extant copies known to be written in the second century, the late documents are actually validating the accuracy of the copying process and thereby strongly suggesting that the original manuscript was basically the same in content. Again, the Gospels have more evidence for trustworthiness than any other ancient writing when assessed in terms of the number of manuscripts. Compared to Homer's *Iliad*, of which only 643 manuscripts are known to have survived, the most of any ancient document, the New Testament has nearly 25,000 manuscripts or portions thereof (including Greek and other languages), spanning fifteen centuries[5] (see tables 2.1 and 2.2). When the content of the New Testament manuscripts emanating from the fifteenth century is compared with the content of those of the second century, no significant textual differences can be documented, indicating the remarkable care that has been exercised over the centuries by the copyists to preserve its message. Sir Frederic Kenyon, late distinguished historian and archeologist and director of the British Museum, makes these compelling remarks regarding the New Testament:

---

[4] Ibid., 60–72.
[5] Ibid. See also Norman L. Geisler, "New Testament Manuscripts," in *Baker Encyclopedia of Christian Apologetics* (Grand Rapids, MI: Baker, 1999), 531–538.

The interval, then, between the dates of original composition and the earliest extant evidence becomes so small as to be in fact negligible, and the last foundation for any doubt that the Scriptures have come down to us substantially as they were written has now been removed. [Thus] both the authenticity and the general integrity of the books of the New Testament may be regarded as finally established.[6]

TABLE 2.2: Surviving Manuscripts for the New Testament

Extant Greek Manuscripts:

Uncials	307
Minuscules	2,860
Lectionaries	2,410
Papyri	109
SUBTOTAL	5,686

Manuscripts in Other Languages:

Latin Vulgate	10,000 plus
Ethiopic	2,000 plus
Slavic	4,101
Armenian	2,587
Syriac Peshitta	350 plus
Bohairic	100
Arabic	75
Old Latin	50
Anglo Saxon	7
Gothic	6
Sogdian	3
Old Syriac	2
Persian	2
Frankish	1
SUBTOTAL	19,284 plus
TOTAL ALL MSS	24,970 plus

Taken from: Josh McDowell, *Evidence for Christianity* (Nashville: Thomas Nelson, 2006), 60–61. (Used by permission of Thomas Nelson.)

---

[6] Frederic G. Kenyon, *The Bible and Archaeology* (New York: Harper & Row, 1940), 288.

A third body of evidence attesting to the trustworthiness of the New Testament Gospels is that related to the *testimony of the early church fathers.* These were men who played significant leadership roles in the early church and were involved with the spread of Christianity in the latter part of the first century and throughout the second to the fourth centuries, but were not involved in the actual writing of the New Testament itself. Examples include Justin Martyr, Origen, Irenaeus, and Eusebius. These early church fathers viewed the Gospels and the other books of the New Testament as reliable and authoritative sources detailing the life and times of Jesus, including his death and resurrection. They often used this scriptural material in their commentaries and sermons. In fact, Norman Geisler and William Nix noted that some 32,000 citations of the New Testament have been unraveled from the patristic sources prior to the Council of Nicaea in 325 AD. If one adds to this the writings of Eusebius, who was a contemporary of this Council, the number exceeds 36,000 quotations.[7] The importance of this remarkable body of quoted material is emphasized by the late Princeton professor and New Testament textual critic Bruce Metzger:

> Indeed, so extensive are these citations that if all other sources for our knowledge of the text of the New Testament were destroyed, they would be sufficient alone for the reconstruction of practically the entire New Testament.[8]

Even though the evidence just presented is compelling, the issue of historical accuracy still must be addressed. The manuscripts we have may be totally reliable and accurate from the standpoint of what the Gospel writers reported, but were those original manuscripts historically accurate? For example, a given writer could have written that Jesus did or said "x, y, and z," when in fact he didn't do or say that at all. Since historical accuracy ultimately is crucial to determining who the "real" Jesus actually was, this issue becomes especially important and cannot be ignored.

---

[7] Norman L. Geisler and William E. Nix, *A General Introduction to the Bible* (Chicago: Moody, 1986), 353–354.
[8] Bruce M. Metzger, *The Text of the New Testament* (New York: Oxford University Press, 1964), 86.

So how do we deal with this concern? A key issue relates to the dating of the Gospels. If they were written in the second century, one would have reason to believe that they could be tainted with legends about Jesus rather than containing actual historical events, since enough time would have elapsed from when Jesus actually lived on earth (he was 33 when he died, probably between AD 30 and 33) for false stories to have been concocted about him. Further, since people who knew Jesus personally would long since have died, there would be no one to challenge these stories. On the other hand, if the Gospels were written in the first century, even in the latter part of it, this would be close enough to the death of Jesus to ensure a more accurate accounting. While conservative scholars date the Synoptic Gospels (i.e., Matthew, Mark and Luke) somewhere around AD 50–75, with Mark being the earliest, followed by Matthew and Luke, even the more liberal scholars agree that the dating is no later than AD 65–90. With the Gospel of John, both groups agree that the dating is no later than AD 95.[9]

Biblical historian and apologist Gary Habermas argues backward from the book of Acts to date the Gospels. He notes:

> Most of this book is occupied with the ministries of Peter and Paul, and much of the action centers in the city of Jerusalem. The martyrdoms of Stephen (7:54–60) and the apostle James (12:1–2) are recorded, and the book concludes with Paul under arrest in Rome (28:14–31). Yet Acts says nothing concerning the deaths of Paul and Peter (mid-60s A.D.) or James, Jesus' brother (about A.D. 62). Moreover, accounts of the Jewish War with the Romans (beginning in A.D. 66) and the fall of Jerusalem (A.D. 70) are also strangely absent. Further, the book ends enigmatically with Paul under house arrest, without any resolution to the situation.
>
> How could the author of Acts not mention these events or resolve Paul's dilemma, each of which is centrally related to the text's crucial themes? These events would even seem to dwarf many of the other recorded occurrences. It is difficult to resist the conclusion that the author did not record these items simply because they had not yet

---

[9] Gary Habermas, "Why I Believe the New Testament Is Historically Reliable," in *Why I Am a Christian*, ed. Norman L. Geisler and Paul K. Hoffman (Grand Rapids, MI: Baker, 2001), see chapter 9.

occurred. These omissions argue persuasively for an early date for the composition of Acts, before the mid-60s A.D.

If it is held that Luke was written prior to Acts but after Mark and Matthew, as perhaps most critical scholars do, then all [four] books may be dated before A.D. 65. It is simply amazing that Acts could be dated A.D. 80–85 [as some scholars have done] and the author not be aware of, or otherwise neglect to mention, any of these events.[10]

If Habermas's "arguing backward from Acts" is valid, as I believe it is, then the Synoptic Gospels were all written prior to AD 65.

It should also be noted that the book of Acts is considered to be a carefully written document, incredibly accurate from a historical standpoint, and the information contained in it has been validated numerous times by archaeology and other external sources irrespective of its basic message concerning Jesus and his gospel.[11] Since it is generally agreed that Luke the physician authored Acts, it would be logical to conclude that the same care he exercised in ensuring its historical accuracy was also employed in telling the story of the early development of Christianity and what its leaders believed concerning Jesus. Further, as Luke is also credited with writing the Gospel associated with his name, it is equally appropriate to conclude that the Gospel of Luke is likewise accurate in its presentation of historical information and its portrayal of the life and ministry of Jesus.[12] Finally, if one compares the picture of Jesus portrayed in Luke's Gospel with that portrayed in the other Gospels, the person who emerges is virtually the same in all four Gospels even though various aspects of his life are painted differently—which should not be surprising since four different people wrote these Gospels. One thing that is identical in each Gospel is that Jesus was viewed as God in fleshly form, who died by crucifixion and rose from the dead three days later.[13]

For those unfamiliar with the New Testament, thirteen of its

[10] Ibid., 149–150 (used with permission from Baker Publishing Group).
[11] Colin Hemer, *The Book of Acts in the Setting of Hellenistic History*, ed. Conrad H. Gempf (Winona Lake, IN: Eisenbrauns, 1990); A. N. Sherwin-White, *Roman Society and Roman Law in the New Testament* (Oxford: Oxford University Press, 1963), see especially chapters 3–5.
[12] McDowell, *Evidence for Christianity*, 91–97.
[13] Richard Bauckham, *Jesus and the Eyewitnesses: The Gospels as Eyewitness Testimony* (Grand Rapids, MI: Eerdmans, 2006).

twenty-seven books are ascribed to the apostle Paul. While his author-ship of a few of these is questioned by some scholars, it is almost uni-versally agreed that he wrote Romans, 1 and 2 Corinthians, Galatians, and Philippians, and very likely 1 Thessalonians and Philemon. This is important because Paul championed the early development of Christianity, and all of his writings are focused on Jesus in one form or another. Thus, as Habermas shows, by studying Paul's books we can learn a great deal about who the historical Jesus really was and what early Christians believed.[14] Using only the books listed above as being authored by Paul, Habermas has summarized three kinds of informa-tion that can be gleaned from Paul's writings concerning Jesus:

> One route is to list the historical data about Jesus—both the events of his life and his teachings—that are specifically found in Paul's accepted epistles. Jesus was born as a Jew (Gal. 3:16) from the family of David (Rom. 1:3) and lived under Jewish law (Gal. 4:4). Jesus had brothers (1 Cor. 9:5), one of whom was James (1 Cor. 15:7), as well as twelve dis-ciples (1 Cor. 15:7). Paul knew that at least some of Jesus' brothers and apostles had wives (1 Cor. 9:5). In fact, Paul knew personally James, as well as apostles Peter and John, having spent time with at least the first two on more than one occasion (Gal. 1:18–2:16).
>
> Paul also relates a few personal qualities about Jesus. He was poor (2 Cor. 8:9), a servant who acted with humility (Phil. 2:5, 7–8), meekness, and gentleness (2 Cor. 10:1). Though he did not act on his own behalf, he was still abused by others (Rom 15:3). Further, Paul also knew a number of Jesus' teachings and encouraged believ-ers to obey them. This is clearly indicated when he specifically refers to Jesus' words (1 Cor. 7:10; 9:14; 11:23–25). A number of times, his point seems to be taken from one of Jesus' sayings in the Gospels. Some of these instances include topics of divorce and remarriage (1 Cor. 7:10–11), ministers being paid wages (1 Cor. 9:14), paying taxes (Rom. 13:6–7), the duty to love our neighbors as we do ourselves (Rom. 13:9), and ceremonial cleanliness (Rom. 14:14). On topics such as women, the treatment of sinners, and society's outcasts, Paul also seems to have been aware of Jesus' attitudes and teaching. His asser-tion about specific titles reflecting Jesus' deity are another important area for comparison with Jesus' own teachings (Rom. 1:3–4; 10:9). Paul also encourages believers to be vigilant in light of Jesus' second

---

[14] Habermas, "Why I Believe the New Testament Is Historically Reliable," 149–155.

coming (1 Thess. 4:15), which would happen like the thief that comes in the night (1 Thess. 5:2–11).

Paul provides the most details concerning the last week of Jesus' life, speaking frequently of these events due to their centrality to the gospel. He gives particulars concerning the Lord's Supper, even citing the words Jesus spoke on this occasion (1 Cor. 11:23–25). Paul speaks often of Jesus' death (Rom. 4:25; 5:8), specifying crucifixion (Rom. 6:6; Gal. 2:20) and mentioning Jewish instigation (1 Thess. 2:14–15). He tells how Jesus was buried, rose again three days later, and appeared to numerous people, both individually and in groups (1 Cor. 15:3–8). He is now at God's right hand (Rom. 8:34).[15]

It should be obvious from these summaries that a considerable amount of valuable information exists in Paul's writings regarding who Jesus was and what was being said about him in the first century. When it is further noted that Paul died (probably by beheading) at the hands of the Romans somewhere around AD 65, this means that the Christian message articulated by him occurred within no more than 35 years following Jesus's death, making it too close to the time he lived among us to be the subject of legend or myth. It is also of note that Paul's interaction with James, the brother of Jesus, as well as with Peter and John, two of his disciples, is but another validation that Paul knew exactly who the "real Jesus" was and based his preaching on that knowledge. Thus, whether one is willing to accept an early dating of the Gospels or not, the body of information regarding Jesus in Paul's epistles more than supports the reliability of these four accounts of his life in general terms and certainly with respect to his death and resurrection.[16] It is this bounty of *information* contained in the New Testament that we know was *written within a brief period following Jesus's death* that provides yet a fourth line of evidence to its credibility. Of particular note, in this regard, is this emphatic statement from the eminent Johns Hopkins University professor William Foxwell Albright, who during his lifetime was considered one of the world's foremost biblical archaeologists—often referred to as the dean of American biblical archaeologists:

---

[15] Ibid., 156–158 (used with permission of Baker Publishing Group).
[16] Ibid.

In my opinion, every book of the New Testament was written by a baptized Jew between the forties and the eighties of the first century (very probably sometime between about AD 50 and 75).[17]

Even more telling is the conclusion of radical liberal theologian John A. T. Robinson, who for most of his professional life believed in a late dating of many of the New Testament books, and especially the Gospels. After a careful re-review of the evidence, which he published in the book *Redating the New Testament,* he boldly affirmed that the whole of the New Testament was written before the fall of Jerusalem in AD 70.[18] This means that the body of information we have available to us concerning Jesus in the Gospel accounts was written within 40 years of his death at the most.[19] This makes it virtually impossible for legend or myth to have crept into these accounts, as eyewitnesses of his life would have still been alive to dispute any falsehood. Thus, we are provided with these four lines of evidence attesting to the reliability of the New Testament—lines that merge to offer an extremely compelling bounty of data defending the trustworthiness of this document and particularly its Gospels.

Challenges to the Truthfulness of the Gospels

Despite the aforementioned arguments, a number of challenges are currently questioning the validity of the Gospel accounts, and whether they give a true picture of the historical Jesus. These challenges have taken many forms, but those which have been given the greatest visibility, due in part to extensive media coverage, are the Jesus Seminar, *The Da Vinci Code* by Dan Brown, and a University of North Carolina religion professor's book by the catchy title *Misquoting Jesus*. So, should we be concerned about these attacks?

---

[17] William Foxwell Albright, interview, "William Albright: Toward a More Conservative View," in *Christianity Today* (January 18, 1963), 3.

[18] John A.T. Robinson, *Redating the New Testament* (Philadelphia: Westminster, 1976).

[19] As clearly noted in the foregoing discussion, the preponderance of evidence strongly suggests that the Synoptic Gospels (Matthew, Mark, and Luke) were written prior to AD 65, and some scholars such as Albright and Robinson also believe that the Gospel of John was written within a similar time frame. Church tradition, as well as most contemporary biblical scholars, espouse a much later dating for John's Gospel, usually around AD 90–95. Even so, this would be only some 60 years after Jesus's death, a time span too short for myth or legend to have influenced its content.

The Jesus Seminar

The Jesus Seminar, founded in the mid-1980s by Robert Funk and John Dominic Crossan, is a group of nonconventional scholars who have challenged the accuracy of the New Testament Gospels and have strongly contested the Jesus that traditional Christianity has worshiped.[20] This group is vehemently opposed to anything supernatural, and accordingly rejects the resurrection (except in some "spiritual" sense), irrespective of whatever evidence is available supporting this event. In their view, the biblical Jesus is totally fallacious, and anyone making him the object of faith is at best misguided. Crossan has gone on record as asserting that Jesus was just "a peasant Jewish cynic."[21] Interestingly, Jesus Seminar scholars have gained a great deal of media exposure in recent years and have appeared on various television documentaries discussing the life of Jesus. To those who are biblically illiterate or only marginally familiar with the claims of historic Christianity, the message of the Jesus Seminar is often very persuasive. I have watched a number of these presentations and can attest to this impression.

But is their radical point of view defensible? As a person of science who firmly believes that decisions must be made and conclusions reached on the basis of solid evidence, I find the dogmatic statements of the Jesus Seminar unconvincing. For example, the scholars associated with this movement uncritically assert that 80 percent or more of the sayings of Jesus in the four Gospels were not spoken by him.[22] They make this determination without any compelling evidence, using instead a voting system employing colored beads to decide which sayings are credible. Since they have a priori ruled out any possibility of the supernatural or miraculous, any saying that even hints at these possibilities is immediately excluded because their preconceived Jesus couldn't possibly have said such a thing. Similarly, if a saying is linked with an action that their Jesus almost certainly would not have done,

---

[20] Geisler, *Baker Encyclopedia of Christian Apologetics*, 386–388.

[21] John Dominic Crossan, *The Historical Jesus: The Life of a Mediterranean Jewish Peasant* (San Francisco: HarperCollins, 1991).

[22] R. W. Funk and R. W. Hoover, eds., *The Five Gospels: The Search for the Authentic Words of Jesus* (Sonoma, CA: Polebridge; New York: Macmillan, 1993).

the saying is again relegated to the unlikely or the impossible. Using their color-coded bead system, they decided which sayings of Jesus were credible. Red beads meant "yes," black beads "no," pink beads "maybe," and gray beads meant that Jesus was not the originator of the saying even though it probably reflected his thinking on a given subject. One can easily see the absurdity of evaluating data in this fashion. It is basically "stacking the deck" so that the results turn out as they want them to. It would be similar to my performing a scientific experiment and excluding any findings that differed from my preconceived notions of what the outcome should be. Nonetheless, the Jesus Seminar continues to push its agenda and has gained incredible exposure through the liberal media. Notwithstanding this reality, the consensus of serious scholarship considers their work non-evidence-based and seriously flawed methodologically.[23]

The Jesus Seminar has also gone on record as saying that there were several "Christianities" in the first century, and the only reason why the New Testament Gospels have enjoyed the preeminence that they have is because certain members of the early church were able to usurp sufficient power so that the "other Gospels" available were not able to gain a fair hearing.[24] The "other Gospels" referred to are a collection of writings about Jesus and his alleged teachings commonly called the "Gnostic Gospels." The name Gnostic comes from the Greek word *gnosis*, which literally means "knowledge." The equivalent English word would be "enlightenment." Most scholars[25] believe that Gnosticism (and hence these Gnostic Gospels) emerged as a reaction to early Christian teaching about the death and resurrection of Jesus and the assertion that Jesus was God incarnate in human flesh. To the Gnostic, Jesus did not come to die for the sins of mankind, but rather to show men and women how to release their spirits (i.e., souls) from the material world and thus experience "true gnosis." Accordingly, salva-

---

[23] N. T. Wright, "Five Gospels but No Gospel: Jesus and the Seminar," in *Authenticating the Activities of Jesus*, ed. Bruce Chilton and Craig A. Evans (Leiden, Netherlands: Brill, 1999), 83–120.
[24] Marvin Meyer, *The Gnostic Gospels of Jesus: The Definitive Collection of Mystical Gospels and Secret Books about Jesus of Nazareth* (New York: HarperCollins, 2005).
[25] John Ankerberg and John Weldon, *The Facts on False Views of Jesus: The Truth behind the Jesus Seminar* (Eugene, OR: Harvest, 1997).

tion has nothing to do with the forgiveness of sins but rather involves discovering one's true self from within and in such discovery finding true happiness.[26] The Jesus Seminar alleges that this alternative Christianity was the true message that Jesus came to teach rather than the message promulgated in the New Testament Gospels. Had the Gnostics been given a fair hearing, the Jesus that we have come to believe is the "real Jesus" would be exposed for what he is, and the Gnostic Jesus would be shown to be the "true Jesus." Similarly, the Gnostic writings, such as the Gospel of Mary, Gospel of Thomas, Gospel of Philip, and Gospel of Judas (more than forty have been found), would now be the true Gospels rather than those contained in the New Testament.

The problem with this line of reasoning is that Gnosticism really did not emerge as a viable movement until the second century and reached its greatest peak from the mid-second century and into the fourth century. Further, its many writings did not appear until the second to the fourth centuries. Although the Jesus Seminar would like us to believe that these writings developed in concurrence with the New Testament Gospels, solid evidence for this notion is simply lacking. In his excellent book *The Hidden Gospels*, Philip Jenkins, professor of history at Pennsylvania State University, has carefully reviewed the history of Gnosticism and its writings and clearly shows that an early dating for these writings is simply not supported by the evidence.[27] Luke Timothy Johnson, Christian historian at Emory University, reaches a similar conclusion in his book *The Real Jesus*.[28] Thus, the New Testament Gospels stand firm as the earliest accounts of who Jesus was, and the Gnostic writings embody a much later movement to challenge this Jesus.

The Da Vinci Code

Equally deceptive in its distortion of historic Christianity and the life and message of Jesus is Dan Brown's *The Da Vinci Code*.[29] Having sold

---

[26] Darrell L Bock, *The Missing Gospels: Unearthing the Truth behind Alternative Christianities* (Nashville: Thomas Nelson, 2006), 32–55.

[27] Philip Jenkins, *Hidden Gospels: How the Search for Jesus Lost Its Way* (New York: Oxford University Press, 2001).

[28] Luke Timothy Johnson, *The Real Jesus: The Misguided Quest for the Historical Jesus and the Traditional Gospels* (New York: HarperCollins, 1996).

[29] Dan Brown, *The Da Vinci Code* (New York: Doubleday, 2003).

in excess of 80 million copies and having been translated into more than 40 languages, this book has probably done more to misrepresent and demean the truth of Christianity than any single publication in recent times. There is no question that Brown is a skilled author and able to develop an intriguing plot, but distinguishing fact from fiction is extremely difficult to do in this book despite his contention that it is only a novel. One can only wonder whether the subject matter was intentionally chosen and deliberately planned to confuse those who possess only a marginal understanding of the New Testament and the claims of Christianity. Even many Christians have been led astray by this book. The number of other books that have been written to contest the message of *The Da Vinci Code* speaks volumes concerning its potentially damaging effect.

It is not the intent of this discussion to provide a comprehensive critique of *The Da Vinci Code*. That has been done by various other authors; accordingly, the reader is referred to such source material.[30] My purpose is to summarize those areas of the book that directly challenge the truthfulness of the Gospels and to emphasize why I do not think this information is valid. To do so, one needs to understand the basic plot of the book. Simply put, the book centers around the claim that Jesus is not the Son of God. Rather, the church has suppressed the actual truth, which was that Jesus married Mary Magdalene and through this union she gave birth to a "sacred" bloodline that would eventually become a medieval family of French kings known as the Merovingian dynasty. Thus, the "Holy Grail" is not the cup used by Jesus at the Last Supper, as the church has alleged; rather, it is Mary Magdalene herself. This being so, the union between Jesus and Mary was meant to establish the worship of "the sacred feminine" and not of Jesus himself. The claim of *The Da Vinci Code* is that this truth was preserved throughout the cen-

---

[30] Excellent resource materials that refute Brown's false claims regarding Christianity include: Erwin Lutzer, *The Da Vinci Deception* (Carol Stream, IL: Tyndale, 2004); Darrell L. Bock, *Breaking the Da Vinci Code* (Nashville: Thomas Nelson, 2004); Greg Jones, *Beyond Da Vinci* (New York: Seabury, 2004); Josh McDowell, *The Da Vinci Code: A Quest for Answers* (Holiday, FL: Green Key, 2006); Hank Hanegraaff and Paul L. Maier, *The Da Vinci Code: Fact or Fiction?* (Carol Stream, IL: Tyndale, 2004).

turies by a secret society even though the church did everything it could to suppress it. Further, Leonardo Da Vinci was part of the means of conveying this secret and used his paintings to reveal it through encrypted codes. Finally, since Jesus was not the Son of God, his death on the cross was final and there was no resurrection as the church has preached.

As interesting and convincing as this plot may be, is there any evidence to support it? The answer is a resounding no. First, the allegation that the church has intentionally misrepresented who Jesus is and suppressed the real truth about him is simply without foundation. We have already reviewed the evidence supporting the reliability of the Gospels, from which the information about Jesus is primarily derived. Dan Brown may choose to disregard this evidence, which he has the right to do, but to accuse the church of suppressing the truth about Jesus as written in the Gospels is simply bogus. It is incumbent on Brown to provide alternative evidence supporting his claims and why he thinks the Gospels are not reliable source material; this he never does, nor to my knowledge has he ever tried to do so.

Second, the claim in *The Da Vinci Code* that Jesus was considered merely a human prior to the Council of Nicaea in AD 325, and was upgraded to "Son of God" status through the emperor Constantine's doing, represents a total misunderstanding of the purpose of that Council. The Council was by no means the first time Jesus was declared to be the Son of God. In the view of the original apostles of Jesus, and later the early church fathers, he always was the Son of God. This was firmly stated in all four Gospels as well as throughout the rest of the New Testament more than a hundred times. While it is true that Jesus was also man, he was never somehow upgraded from "man" to "Son of God." He was the God-man, fully God and fully man. The issue for the Council of Nicaea was not whether Jesus became the Son of God but whether his nature as God was equal with that of God the Father. The decision reached was that Jesus was always the Son of God and always equal with God the Father. Further, Constantine had nothing to do with this decision but simply appointed the bishops who made up the Council. Finally, the vote that gave rise to this decision was not a close one as Dan Brown alleged, but was at least 218 in favor and only 2 opposed.[31]

The third issue with regard to *The Da Vinci Code* is the marital status of Jesus. Despite any claims to the contrary, there is not a shred of evidence that Jesus was ever married, let alone to Mary Magdalene. One would think that at least some reference to his marital status would be recorded somewhere if indeed he was married. Yet we find no record of any such assertion in the Gospels, anywhere else in the New Testament, in the writings of the early church fathers, or even in the Gnostic Gospels. For Dan Brown to state that this is a matter of "historical record" places the burden of proof on him. As regards Mary Magdalene, she is not disdained in the Gospels or by the church, as Brown alleges. In the Gospels, after having had seven demons cast out, she became a close follower of Jesus and is mentioned as being the first witness to Jesus's resurrection and the first to announce to the apostles that Jesus had indeed risen from the dead. Further, in the Catholic Church she is honored as a saint. Nowhere, however, is there any reference to her being romantically involved with Jesus.

On the above issues alone, it should be clear that Dan Brown frequently mixes fantasy and fact so that the reader has great difficulty in distinguishing the two. As a source book for historical Christianity, *The Da Vinci Code* comes up wanting.

Misquoting Jesus

A somewhat different assault on the veracity of the New Testament Gospels is articulated in the recent book *Misquoting Jesus*.[32] The book is authored by religion professor Bart Ehrman of the University of North Carolina at Chapel Hill. He contends that the reliability of

---

[31] Mark Shea, Edward Sri, and Editors of the Catholic Exchange, *The Da Vinci Deception* (West Chester, PA: Ascension Press, 2006), 65–68; additional information about the Council of Nicaea can be found in Mark A. Noll, *Turning Points: Decisive Moments in the History of Christianity* (Grand Rapids, MI: Baker, 1997), 47–64.

[32] Bart D. Ehrman, *Misquoting Jesus: The Story behind Who Changed the Bible and Why* (New York: HarperCollins, 2006).

the Gospels is open to serious question due to the multiple errors that have been introduced into the text by the copyists (i.e., scribes). For example, a text originally written in the first century is likely to have been copied many times over down through the centuries. During the repeated copying, errors are virtually guaranteed due to human imperfection alone. Further, Ehrman asserts, presumptions, presuppositions, and prejudices on the part of the copyist when confronted with something missing from the text being copied are likely to introduce additional errors as the copyist simply fills in what he thinks is missing. It is Ehrman's estimate that as many as 200,000 to 400,000 errors may have been introduced into the Gospel texts in this way. Such being the case, it is entirely likely from his perspective that the texts we have regarding the life of Jesus are quite different from what the original manuscripts intended to convey.

On the surface, Ehrman's concern is quite legitimate. After all, if there really are this many errors, can the Gospels be trusted? Having edited several textbooks myself, I am well aware of the importance of accuracy and the way that misplaced words, substituted phrases, or deleted textual material can greatly alter the meaning of a manuscript. Nevertheless, it must be stressed that all errors are not equal. If substitutions such as "man" for "mankind," "a" for "the," "right" for "rite," or "whole" for "hole" were used, most readers could figure out the intended meaning by reading the affected sentence in the context of the paragraph in which it was placed. On the other hand, substitutions such as "adult" for "theater," "donkey" for "car," or "house" for "mountain" would be much more difficult to reconcile and more likely to alter the meaning of the original text. Thus, in assessing the seriousness of the errors Ehrman encountered, one must analyze them in the context of where they occurred and how the intended meaning might have been influenced. Depending on the outcome of such an analysis, the altered manuscript resulting from the copying process may not be substantially different from its original counterpart.

So how serious are the errors that Ehrman claims exist? Despite his insistence that they undermine the veracity of the Gospels, most scholars who work in the area of textual criticism are not as convinced. Ben Witherington III, considered one of the top contemporary New Testament scholars, agrees that there are many New Testament textual variants, but he vehemently challenges Ehrman that any essential Christian doctrine has been "cooked up after the fact" and then made to look like it was part of the corpus of original Christian belief. He boldly asserts that the virgin birth, the Trinity (and thus Jesus's deity), and the crucifixion and bodily resurrection of Jesus were key Christian beliefs from the beginning of the Christian church and not ideas added later through manuscript copying errors. This conclusion by Ehrman "is simply false," Witherington argues.[33]

New Testament textual critic Daniel Wallace, from The Center for the Study of New Testament Manuscripts, in Dallas, comes to a similar conclusion. In analyzing Ehrman's arguments, he offers some interesting insights.[34] First, he notes that 70 to 80 percent of the textual variants with which Ehrman is concerned are no more than spelling differences that have no impact on meaning. Second, there are nonsense errors where the copyist was inattentive and the resultant mistake was obvious, so that the right word could be easily reconstituted. Third, there are synonym variants such as substituting the word "Jesus" for "Lord" or vice versa. Fourth, there are variants that cannot even be translated into English because our language is not as highly inflected as the Greek language; despite this circumstance, the meaning is totally unaffected. In summarizing his thoughts about *Misquoting Jesus*, Wallace offers these comments:

> The remarkable thing is you go through his whole book and you say, Where did he actually prove anything? Ehrman didn't prove that *any* doctrine is jeopardized. Let me repeat the basic thesis that has been argued since [the year] 1707: *No cardinal or essential doctrine is altered by any textual variant that has plausibility of going back to the original.* The evidence for that has not changed to this day.[35]

---

[33] Ben Witherington III, *What Have They Done with Jesus?* (New York: HarperCollins, 2006), 7.
[34] See Lee Strobel, *The Case for the Real Jesus* (Grand Rapids, MI: Zondervan, 2007), 65–100. This reference involves an extensive discussion between Strobel and Wallace regarding the book *Misquoting Jesus*; see also: Daniel B. Wallace, "The Gospel according to Bart," *Journal of the Evangelical Theological Society* 49 (June 2006): 327–349.
[35] Quoted in Strobel, *Case for the Real Jesus*, 88–89.

The most comprehensive discussion of *Misquoting Jesus* of which I am aware is Timothy Paul Jones's *Misquoting Truth*, with the interesting subtitle *A Guide to the Fallacies of Bart Ehrman's Misquoting Jesus.*[36] In a point by point analysis, Jones dismantles Ehrman's logic and shows in a compelling way that virtually every argument Ehrman presents to challenge the reliability of the New Testament, and especially the Gospels, simply does not hold up under rigorous scrutiny. As an example, Jones comprehensively reviews several dozen passages which Ehrman claims have been radically altered by copying errors so that the original intent and/or message has been significantly obscured. Jones convincingly shows that Ehrman grossly overestimates the significance of these variations, and that in the end at least 99 percent of them "stem from differences in spelling, word order, or the relationships between nouns and definite articles—variants that are easily recognizable and, in most cases, virtually unnoticeable in translations."[37] In responding to Ehrman's allegations that widely held beliefs such as the divinity of Jesus, the Trinity, and the divine origin of the Bible itself stem from both intentional and accidental alterations by scribes, Jones makes these observations:

> As I examine *Misquoting Jesus*, I find nothing that measures up to the title. . . . What I find is a great deal of discussion about a handful of textual variants—none of which ultimately changes any essential belief that's presented in the New Testament. What's more, despite the sensational title of *Misquoting Jesus*, I find only a half-dozen times when Jesus *might* have been misquoted, and most of these supposed changes simply echo ideas that are found elsewhere in Scripture.[38]

Finally, Jones also presents compelling evidence that the Gospels are eyewitness accounts of what they report about Jesus; were written by Matthew, Mark, Luke, and John as Christian tradition has alleged for the past two thousand years; and were accepted by the early church as reliable sources not because of some political power

---

[36] Timothy Paul Jones, *Misquoting Truth: A Guide to the Fallacies of Bart Ehrman's Misquoting Jesus* (Downers Grove, IL: InterVarsity Press, 2007).
[37] Ibid., 43–44.
[38] Ibid., 77.

play that prevented the Gnostic Gospels from being given a fair hearing, but because these latter writings did not appear on the historical scene until much later than the Gospels and were considered heretical because they presented a Jesus different from the Jesus presented by those who were eyewitnesses to his earthly ministry.[39] All of these beliefs Ehrman attempts to impugn in *Misquoting Jesus*, but the logic behind his arguments simply does not measure up to the evidence provided in *Misquoting Truth*.

Perhaps the most telling challenge to *Misquoting Jesus* are the comments of Bruce M. Metzger, whom we met earlier in this chapter. Metzger, who actually mentored Ehrman in his doctoral work at Princeton, was interviewed by Lee Strobel when Metzger was eighty-three years old. Strobel summarizes that interview in his book *The Case for the Real Jesus*. Asked whether he believed that variations in biblical manuscripts "tend to be minor rather than substantive," Metzger replied, "Yes, that's correct. . . . The more significant variations do not overthrow any doctrine of the church."[40] When asked how his study of the New Testament text affected his personal faith, Metzger added:

> Oh, . . . it has increased the basis of my personal faith to see the firmness with which these materials have come down to us. . . . I've asked questions all my life, I've dug into the text, I've studied this thoroughly, and today I know with confidence that my trust in Jesus has been well placed.[41]

It is evident from these statements that Metzger had a high regard for the New Testament and its trustworthiness and was not dissuaded by textual variants as his former student seems to have been. Thus, it would seem that Ehrman has drastically overstated his case.

Concluding Thoughts

It has been the intent of this chapter to consider the evidence both for and against the reliability of the New Testament Gospels as source

[39] Ibid., 95–137.
[40] Quoted in Strobel, *Case for the Real Jesus*, 99.
[41] Ibid.

material for gaining knowledge about Jesus and particularly about his death and resurrection. While you will ultimately have to decide how you think the evidence stacks up, keep in mind that if you use the same standards to evaluate the trustworthiness of the New Testament as are used to evaluate other ancient documents, the New Testament is every bit as reliable as these other writings, if not more so. I am of the personal persuasion that the preponderance of evidence overwhelmingly supports the veracity of the New Testament and especially the Gospels. In my judgment the methodology of the Jesus Seminar is so flawed and its liberal agenda so intent on promoting a point of view that flies in the face of alternative challenges that it is not worthy of any serious consideration. Similarly, *The Da Vinci Code*, clearly an interesting novel with an intriguing plot, presents a Jesus that simply cannot be validated historically. Finally, *Misquoting Jesus*, while presenting a very readable analysis of textual criticism and how it is used to decipher the reliability of ancient documents such as the New Testament, overstates the significance of textual variants in New Testament manuscripts—as though nothing of what the New Testament says can be trusted and the "real Jesus" of the Gospels can never be discovered. As pointed out by Metzger and other New Testament scholars, nothing could be further from the truth.

It seems appropriate, then, to conclude this discussion with the words of Frederick F. Bruce, who was Rylands Professor of Biblical Criticism and Exegesis at the University of Manchester. Bruce offered these thoughts in his classic work *The New Testament Documents: Are They Reliable?*

> The earliest preachers of the gospel knew the value of . . . first-hand testimony, and appealed to it time and again. "We are witnesses of these things," was their constant and confident assertion. And it can have been by no means so easy as some writers seem to think to invent words and deeds of Jesus in those early years, when so many of His disciples were about, who could remember what had and had not happened. . . .
> And it was not only friendly eyewitnesses that the early preachers had to reckon with; there were others less well disposed who were also conversant with the main facts of the ministry and death of Jesus. The

disciples could not afford to risk inaccuracies (not to speak of wilful manipulation of the facts), which would at once be exposed by those who would be only too glad to do so. On the contrary, one of the strong points in the original apostolic preaching is the confident appeal to the knowledge of the hearers; they not only said, "We are witnesses of these things," but also, "As you yourselves also know" (Acts 2:22). Had there been any tendency to depart from the facts in any material respect, the possible presence of hostile witnesses in the audience would have served as a further corrective.[42]

---

[42] F. F. Bruce, *The New Testament Documents: Are They Reliable?* 6th ed. (Downers Grove, IL: Inter-Varsity Press; Grand Rapids, MI: Eerdmans, 1981), 42–43.

3

DID JESUS REALLY DIE BY CRUCIFIXION?

Tantamount to any discussion of a resurrection is the need to determine whether Jesus actually died by crucifixion. If his death did not occur, then any consideration of a resurrection is moot. In reading the biblical accounts of this death in the four Gospels, though, it should be obvious to anyone who pursues this exercise seriously that each Gospel writer was absolutely convinced that Jesus was dead when removed from the cross (see Matthew 27; Mark 15; Luke 23; and John 19). It should be further noted that the detailed account of the early history of Christianity as recorded in the book of Acts refers to Jesus's death dozens of times, not in some "maybe" or "possible" way, but as an established historical fact. Finally, Josephus and Tacitus, two historians who lived in the first century and had no vested interest in Jesus's life and death from a personal perspective, commented on the public execution of Jesus by crucifixion in their writings as though there was no debate regarding the historicity of this event.

The contributions of these two men should not go unnoticed. Among scholars, Josephus is considered an extremely important first-century historian.[1] Born in AD 37, and a Jew himself, his writings about the Jewish people have proved very valuable in providing information about first-century Judaism, particularly about the interactions between the Jewish people and the Romans. His accounts of the Jewish-Roman War between AD 66 and 74 are considered very accurate. In his *Testimonium Flavianum*, he writes about Jesus. The following passage comments on Jesus's crucifixion:

---

[1] Lee Strobel, *The Case for Christ* (Grand Rapids, MI: Zondervan, 1998), 77–81.

> About this time there lived Jesus, a wise man, if indeed one ought to call him a man. For he was one who wrought surprising feats and was a teacher of such people as accept the truth gladly. He won over many Jews and many of the Greeks. He was the Messiah. When Pilate, upon hearing him accused by men of the highest standing amongst us, had condemned him to be crucified, those who had in the first place come to love him did not give up their affection for him. On the third day he appeared to them restored to life, for the prophets of God had prophesied these and countless other marvelous things about him. And the tribe of Christians, so called after him, has still to this day not disappeared.[2]

Various critics have attempted to undermine the importance and authenticity of this passage from Josephus. Edwin Yamauchi of Miami University in Ohio, a biblical archaeologist and expert in the social and cultural history of first-century Christianity, has reviewed the evidence both for and against its authenticity and has concluded that "there's a remarkable consensus among both Jewish and Christian scholars that the passage as a whole is authentic."[3] Thus, this passage provides powerful support, outside the Gospel accounts themselves, that Jesus was a real historical figure who died by crucifixion and presumably came back to life three days later.

Of equal note are the writings of Tacitus (born c. 56 AD), the most important Roman historian of the first century. Being born and reared a Jew, it is not surprising that Jesus would be discussed by Josephus, but for a Roman of Tacitus's stature to comment on Jesus is exceedingly important considering the overall disregard that Romans had for the Jewish people.[4] In his accounts of Nero's persecution of the early Christians for allegedly setting Rome on fire in AD 64, Tacitus had this to say:

> Nero fastened the guilt and inflicted the most exquisite tortures on a class hated for their abominations, called Christians by the populace.

---

[2] Josephus, *Antiquities* 18:63–64.
[3] Cited in Strobel, *Case for Christ*, 79; see also Edwin Yamauchi, "Jesus Outside the New Testament: What Is the Evidence?" in *Jesus Under Fire*, ed. Michael J. Wilkins and J. P. Moreland (Grand Rapids, MI: Zondervan, 1995), 207–230.
[4] Jerry L. Daniel, "Anti-Semitism in the Hellenistic-Roman Period," *Journal of Biblical Literature* 98 (1979): 45–64.

Christus, from whom the name had its origin, suffered the extreme penalty during the reign of Tiberius at the hand of one of our procurators, Pontius Pilatus, and a most mischievous superstition, thus checked for the moment, again broke out not only in Judaea, the first source of the evil, but even in Rome. . . . Accordingly, an arrest was first made of all who pleaded guilty; then, upon their information an immense multitude was convicted, not so much of the crime of firing the city, as of hatred against mankind.[5]

Yamauchi believes that this might be the most important reference to Jesus (i.e., Christus) outside the New Testament. He says,

. . . it does provide us with a very remarkable fact, which is this: crucifixion was the most abhorrent fate that anyone could undergo, and the fact that there was a movement based on a crucified man has to be explained.

How can you explain the spread of a religion based on the worship of a man who had suffered the most ignominious death possible? Of course, the Christian answer is that he was resurrected. Others have to come up with some alternative theory if they don't believe that. But none of the alternative views, to my mind, are very persuasive.[6]

The Swoon Theory

Despite the compelling nature of the New Testament accounts regarding Jesus's death and its corroboration by these first-century historians, some scholars have suggested that Jesus did not really die on the cross but simply became unconscious from the physical and emotional trauma associated with the crucifixion, and when placed in the tomb revived from its cool, moist air.[7] Thus, what has been called a resurrection was not such an event at all, but simply a resuscitation, with Jesus appearing to his disciples and friends—after being revived—in the same mortal body in which he allegedly died.

The *swoon theory*, as this proposed scenario has been called, has surfaced in various books and pamphlets since the nineteenth century and has been put forward by its proponents as a challenge to the his-

---

[5] Tacitus, *Annals* 15.44.
[6] Cited in Strobel, *Case for Christ*, 82–83.
[7] Ibid., 192–193.

toricity of the resurrection.[8] One of the more interesting variations of this theory is that proposed by the late Hugh Schonfield, a Jewish scholar who was a professor of New Testament at the University of Glasgow. In his 1965 book *The Passover Plot*,[9] Schonfield reasoned that Jesus became aware early in life that he was the promised Messiah and as such conducted his life and subsequent death to comply with the Jewish teachings underlying that promise. When it came time for him to die, he arranged for it to happen a few hours before the beginning of the Sabbath so that he would not remain on the cross for an excessive period of time. Worked out in conjunction with Joseph of Arimathea (see next chapter), a close friend and well-connected supporter, the plan was for Joseph to acquire the body of Jesus and remove it from the cross while it was still alive, even though seeming to be dead, and secretly to nurse him back to life. This would give the appearance of a resurrection. Unfortunately this plan went awry when a spear was unexpectedly thrust into Jesus's side, resulting in his death. The important point to remember, though, is that Schonfield firmly believed that, had the spearing not occurred, Jesus would have survived the crucifixion and would have been alive when placed in the tomb. The popularity of this book was such that it was adapted into a movie by the same name in 1976.

More recent versions of the swoon theory, in which the authors do not believe that Jesus was dead when taken down from the cross, appear in the 1982 book *Holy Blood, Holy Grail*, by Baigent, Leigh, and Lincoln; *Jesus and the Riddle of the Dead Sea Scrolls*, by Thiering in 1992; and *The Jesus Papers*, by Baigent in 2006.[10] In all these books, the underlying theme with respect to the crucifixion is that Jesus somehow survived this brutal means of execution and was able to reappear in a fully resuscitated form.

So who is right? Was Jesus really dead when placed in the tomb, or

---

[8] Ibid.

[9] Hugh J. Schonfield, *The Passover Plot* (New York: Bernard Geis Associates [distributed by Random House], 1965).

[10] Michael Baigent, Richard Leigh, and Henry Lincoln, *Holy Blood, Holy Grail* (New York: Delacorte, 1982); Barbara Thiering, *Jesus and the Riddle of the Dead Sea Scrolls: Unlocking the Secrets of His Life Story* (San Francisco: Harper San Francisco, 1992); Michael Baigent, *The Jesus Papers* (San Francisco: Harper San Francisco, 2006).

did it just appear that way? To answer these questions, a careful look at the crucifixion and its brutality is absolutely essential. If Jesus really survived this means of death, it logically follows that the resurrection was and continues to be nothing more than a theological hoax perpetrated on "gullible" individuals by the organized church. But what do we know about the process of crucifixion, and can a human body withstand the horrors of this form of execution?

Death by Crucifixion

Standard means of execution in modern times include the electric chair, lethal injection, firing squad, gas chamber, beheading, and hanging. While each of these methods possesses a certain grotesqueness, common among them is the speed with which they are carried out and the quickness of the resultant death. While varying degrees of pain are experienced by the victim, it is short-lived and generally limited to a few seconds or at most several minutes. Death by crucifixion, in contrast, was designed for maximal pain, prolonged suffering, public humiliation, and a slow, horrendous demise.[11] Despite the belief by some that one can survive this form of execution, its brutality was never intended to provide that option. People condemned to this form of death were never removed from the cross until it was assured that they had died, and they were often left hanging on the cross to be consumed by birds of prey. Sometimes vultures would actually begin eating people who were still alive.

Although its beginnings are uncertain, most scholars believe that crucifixion as a common method of execution originated with the Persians and dates back as early as the sixth century BC.[12] Alexander the Great is reputed to have used this form of execution for the more than two thousand who survived his siege of Tyre.[13] The Romans appear to have learned this technique from the Carthaginians, who

---

[11] Martin Hengel, *Crucifixion in the Ancient World and the Folly of the Message of the Cross* (Philadelphia: Fortress, 1977).

[12] Hengel, *Crucifixion in the Ancient World*; Frederick T. Zugibe, *The Crucifixion of Jesus: A Forensic Inquiry* (New York: M. Evans, 2005); William D. Edwards, Wesley J. Gabel, and Floyd E. Hosmer, "On the Physical Death of Jesus Christ," *Journal of the American Medical Association* 255 (1986): 1455–1463.

[13] Zugibe, *Crucifixion of Jesus*, 52.

were known throughout the ancient world for their macabre methods of torture. When used in the Roman empire, crucifixion was reserved almost exclusively for noncitizens who fell under the categories of hardened criminals, political or religious agitators, and those committing high treason.[14] Occasionally slaves who attempted to obtain their freedom were also executed in this way. The only time that Roman citizens were subjected to crucifixion was when they were convicted of treason or crimes against the state.[15] It should be obvious that the brutality of this method of torture and execution (as discussed below) was a great deterrent against committing such crimes. Of further note, the word "excruciating" (meaning "out of the crucifixion") was the Latin word coined to describe the pain experienced from this form of execution.

The Crucifixion of Jesus

The most famous person in history to have died by crucifixion was Jesus. Regardless of what you may personally think of him, the biblical account of his final hours prior to and including the crucifixion is quite telling and consistent with what has been learned from other sources about this method of torture. A review of that horrific event should forever silence any speculation that Jesus was still alive when placed in the tomb.

Physical and Emotional Abuse Prior to the Crucifixion

The last night of Jesus's life prior to being crucified was one of enormous emotional stress and physical abuse. When assessing the psychophysical trauma that Jesus experienced during the hours preceding the crucifixion, it is not surprising that his life was snuffed out in a few short hours after his being nailed to the cross. Since discussions of Jesus's death are often confined to the crucifixion itself, it is appropriate to review the events of the long night that elapsed before his final execution.

Jesus was arrested in the garden of Gethsemane by the temple guard around midnight following his betrayal by Judas Iscariot. Prior

---

[14] Hengel, *Crucifixion in the Ancient World*; Zugibe, *Crucifixion of Jesus*; Edwards et al., "On the Physical Death of Jesus Christ."
[15] Zugibe, *Crucifixion of Jesus*; Edwards et al., "On the Physical Death of Jesus Christ."

to the arrest, he clearly was under great emotional stress. He prayed three times that the death he knew he was to undergo might be halted if possible, but in the end he was in complete subjection to God's will. The magnitude of this stress was emphasized by the physician Luke in his Gospel where it was pointed out that Jesus perspired "great drops of blood" (Luke 22:42–44). This condition, known as hematidrosis, is a rare dermatologic disorder that can occur in an individual subjected to severe mental distress. Resulting from hemorrhage into the sweat glands, the condition can cause the skin to become quite friable and sensitive to touch. Forensic pathologist Frederick Zugibe, who has written extensively on the medical aspects of the crucifixion, makes these comments regarding hematidrosis:

> The severe mental anxiety due to a profound fear of His prescient sufferings activated the sympathetic nervous system to invoke the stress-fight or flight reaction to such a degree causing hemorrhage of the vessels supplying the sweat glands into the ducts of the sweat glands and extruding out onto the skin. While hematidrosis has been reported to occur from other rare medical entities, the presence of profound fear accounted for a significant number of reported cases including cases in men condemned to execution, . . . occurring during the London blitz, . . . involving a fear of being raped, a fear of a storm while sailing etc. . . . The hematidrosis is a reflection of the severity of Jesus' mental suffering. The effects on the body is that of weakness and mild to moderate dehydration from the severe anxiety and both the blood and sweat loss.[16]

After his arrest, Jesus was immediately subjected to a series of six interrogations that began around one o'clock in the morning and continued until soon after daybreak, when Pilate sentenced him to death. It must be remembered that Jesus probably had little to no opportunity for rest or sleep, with each trial following in rapid succession from the previous one. Thus, the mental and physical abuse which he received was compounded by sleepless exhaustion. The first trial took place with Annas, who had been high priest from AD 6 to 15 and

---

[16] Frederick T. Zugibe, "Forensic and Clinical Knowledge of the Practice of Crucifixion" (Turin Lecture, 2000), 2, http://www.e-forensicmedicine.net.Turin2000.htm (I am indebted to Dr. Zugibe for permission to use this quote).

was the father-in-law of Caiaphas, the current high priest. Jesus was bound and brought before Annas for interrogation regarding his disciples and his teaching (see John 18:12–14, 19–23). Nothing significant came from the questioning, but one of the officials struck Jesus in the face for presumably being sarcastic in the way he answered questions.

Still bound, Jesus was next led away to the house of Caiaphas, the reigning high priest. At this interrogation, the assembled chief priests and the Sanhedrin (sometimes called the "council"), the Jewish supreme court, sought to obtain evidence that Jesus was blaspheming God by claiming to be the promised Messiah (i.e., Christ), the Son of God. The men guarding Jesus abused him by mocking and beating him. They spit on him and berated him by blindfolding him and continued with insults and questions (see John 18:22; Matt. 26:57–68; Mark 14:53–65; Luke 22:54, 63–64).

We do not know where Jesus was taken after this initial meeting with Caiaphas, but at daybreak the council was reconvened and Jesus was again led before them. As previously, Jesus was questioned regarding who he was, and for a second time he claimed to be the Son of God. Thus the council concluded that he deserved to be put to death for blasphemy (see Luke 22:66–71; Matt. 27:1–2; Mark 15:1; John 18:28).

Shortly after this third trial, Jesus was bound again and led away to be handed over to Pilate, the Roman governor who ruled over Judea, for a fourth interrogation (see Luke 23:1–6). Since the Jewish leadership knew that, under Roman law, blasphemy would not "hold water" as a legitimate cause to execute Jesus, they concocted a series of allegations that hopefully would be perceived as direct threats to the Roman government. Accordingly, they claimed that Jesus was subversive, opposed paying taxes to Caesar, and was parlaying himself to be the King of the Jews—and thus was in direct defiance of Caesar's rule and authority. Although Pilate questioned Jesus about his kingly role and what that meant, he was not at all convinced that Jesus was any real threat. Learning that Jesus was from Galilee, Pilate saw this as an opportunity to avoid having to deal with him, and so he sent him to Herod Antipas, who happened to be in Jerusalem at the time, reasoning that Jesus was under Herod's jurisdiction as governor of Galilee (see Luke 23:7–12).

Accordingly, Jesus is interrogated for a fifth time. Like Pilate, Herod is not convinced that Jesus is any significant threat, even though the observing chief priests and teachers of the law continue to abuse him. Nevertheless, Herod and his soldiers mock Jesus as well and then send him back to Pilate, dressed in an elegant robe in derision of his alleged kingship. For a second time (this being the sixth trial), Pilate informs the Jewish leadership that he finds no legitimate basis to bring charges against Jesus. In an interesting compromise, he indicates that he will punish Jesus and then release him. After a series of verbal exchanges with the chief priests, who were stirring up the crowd to demand that Jesus be put to death, Pilate attempted to appease them by having Jesus flogged (see Luke 23:13–22; John 18:29–19:1; Matt. 27:11–26; Mark 15:2–15).

The brutality of this latter treatment must not go unnoticed. Flogging (also called scourging) was a familiar form of intense physical abuse in the first century and appears to have originated in ancient Egypt. The Romans used flogging as a means of interrogating a prisoner as well as to inflict severe physical trauma prior to a person's execution.[17] The unfortunate victim receiving this method of torture was stripped of any clothing and secured to a post or frame with the hands tied around it, allowing the exposed back, buttocks, and legs to be repeatedly beaten (see figure 3.1). The instrument of torture was a rod or whip, the thongs of which were weighted with pieces of bone or metal fragments to make the resultant blow as excruciatingly painful as possible. The severity of the flogging and the number of blows administered was generally left to the whim of the soldier (called *lictor*) performing the torture. Often two lictors would alternate the flogging. The intention of this type of torture was to weaken the victim to the point of fainting, just short of actual death. Experience with such torture demonstrated that thirty-nine blows was the most that could be given and still be compatible with life.[18] How many blows Jesus received is not recorded in the Gospels, but the apostle Peter indicates

---

[17] Edwards et al., "On the Physical Death of Jesus Christ," 1457–1458.
[18] Robert Bucklin, "The Legal and Medical Aspects of the Trial and Death of Christ," *Medicine, Science, and the Law* 10 (1970): 14–26.

that the flogging was especially harsh (see 1 Pet. 2:24), suggesting that the maximum number of blows was employed. Appreciating the method and purpose of flogging, it should come as no surprise that the resultant lacerations and deep contusions induced by the bone and metal fragments would have a ripping effect that would cut deeply into the skin and the subcutaneous tissues. Not infrequently, the torn tissues would extend to the level of the muscles. The net effect of this severe wounding would be horrendous pain and considerable blood loss involving substantial areas of the back, buttocks, and legs. If the blood loss was excessive, as it commonly was, the adverse effect on the remaining blood available in the victim's body to adequately perfuse the vital organs could be considerable. This condition medically is called "hemorrhagic shock."

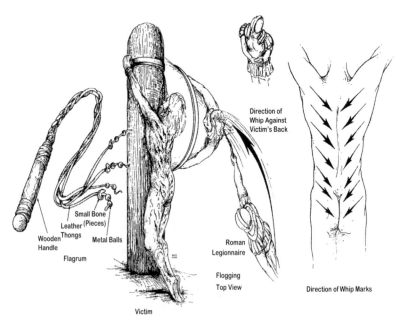

Fig. 3.1: *Scourging.* Left: short whip (*flagrum*) with lead balls and sheep bones tied into leather thongs. Center left: naked victim tied to flogging post. Deep stripe-like lacerations were usually associated with considerable blood loss. Center right: view from above, showing position of lictors. Right: infero-medial direction of wounds.

Taken from William D. Edwards, Wesley J. Gabel, and Floyd E. Hosmer, "On the Physical Death of Jesus Christ," *Journal of the American Medical Association* 255/11 (March 21, 1986): 1457. Used with permission of Mayo Foundation for Medical Education and Research.

Flogging results in extreme weakness, difficulty breathing due to injury to the chest wall (resulting in poor oxygen delivery to tissues), excessive fatigue, and the feeling of wanting to "pass out." If an individual like this were brought to a modern hospital emergency room, he would immediately be admitted to an intensive care unit, treated with intravenous fluids and blood transfusions, given oxygen support, and provided with aggressive wound care to prevent continued bleeding. Survival would depend on whether these adverse derangements could be reversed.

This is the state in which Jesus found himself after the flogging. Apparently amused by his debilitated condition, the Roman soldiers mocked him further by placing a scarlet robe on his bruised, naked body, twisting a crown of thorns on his head, and placing a wooden staff in his right hand to signify his kingship. And as if this were not enough, they continued to spit on him and strike him on the head (see Matt. 27:27–30; Mark 15:16–19; John 19:2–5). Zugibe again has some interesting comments, regarding the crown of thorns:

> The physical effects of the . . . closely spaced thorns would most likely cause trigeminal neuralgia (tic douloureux) due to irritation of the ophthalmic branch of the trigeminal nerve (fifth nerve) and branches of the greater occipital nerves which supply sensory innervation to the front and back of the head region, respectively. This is characterized by severe, lancinating, paroxysmal, electric shock-like pains across the face lasting from seconds to minutes with intermittent refractory periods. Trigger zones are common in various areas of the face which trigger episodes of shooting pains across the head region if touched and is difficult to treat medically. . . . The severe pain would be added to the depth of imminent traumatic shock now developing from the scourging.[19]

Thinking that these tokens of brutality might somehow soften the people's hearts, Pilate again tries to release Jesus and declares his innocence, but to no avail. The chief priests and scribes continue to badger Pilate, insisting that Jesus must be put to death. Ultimately, the pressure is more than he can bear, and Pilate washes his hands of any further responsibility concerning Jesus's fate; he orders that crucifix-

---

[19] Zugibe, "Forensic and Clinical Knowledge of the Practice of Crucifixion," 4 (I am indebted to Dr. Zugibe for permission to use this quote).

ion be carried out as the angry crowd requests (see Luke 23:23–25; John 19:12–16).

The Brutality of Golgotha

With the decision having been sealed that Jesus must be crucified, events rapidly unfolded. He was quickly stripped of the robe he was wearing and probably of any other clothing, to inflict the most egregious degree of humiliation. In removing these garments, the raw skin and lacerated tissue from the flogging was again aggravated, resulting in more paroxysms of pain and bleeding.

The next challenge facing Jesus was the long walk from Pilate's palace to Golgotha, commonly called the Place of the Skull, where the crucifixion would actually take place. This distance was at least a half mile, depending on the route taken. As was customary for victims condemned to crucifixion, Jesus was expected to carry the crossbar (called the *patibulum*), to which his hands would ultimately be nailed, on his shoulders.[20] This crosspiece could weigh anywhere from 75 to 125 pounds and was placed across the nape of the victim's neck and balanced across the outstretched arms, to which it was tied (see figure 3.2).

The weight of this *patibulum* should not go unnoticed. As a comparison, consider bags of fertilizer, which weigh between 25 and 40 pounds each, depending on their composition and density. With my wife being an avid gardener, it is not unusual for me to purchase 15 to 20 bags two or three times yearly and then have to unload them from my SUV. At the time of unloading I usually have to carry them no more than 30 to 50 feet, and often with the assistance of a wheelbarrow. The prospect of having to carry even a 25-pound bag (let alone a heavier one) a half mile is unthinkable, and I am in generally good health. Consider the challenge of carrying a 75- to 125-pound *patibulum* this distance under normal conditions, not to mention having a critically abused body as Jesus did. Little wonder that he was not able to carry this crossbar, and Simon the Cyrenian was delegated to do it for him (see Matt. 27:32; Mark 15:21; Luke 23:26).

---

[20] Edwards et al., "On the Physical Death of Jesus Christ," 1459.

Once Jesus and the military guard assigned to him reached Golgotha, he was quickly thrust to the ground on his back, with the *patibulum* placed under his shoulders and outstretched arms. The next event was to nail his hands to the crossbar. The kind of nails used to impale Christ to the cross are known, through archaeological digs, to actually be spikes measuring approximately 5–7 inches in length and 3/8 inch in their greatest width at the square base.[21] Similar to railroad spikes, they are wide at the top and taper throughout their length (see figure 3.3). The precise entry point on the hands remains debatable. This relates to at least three issues including the definition of "hand," the portion of the hand that would be strong enough to support the body of an individual, and the Scripture referring to Jesus directly, in which it was noted that no bone in his body was broken (i.e., fractured) during the crucifixion (see John 19:36).

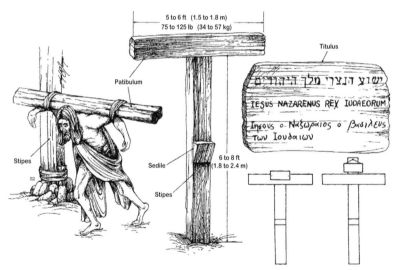

Fig. 3.2: *Cross and titulus.* Left: victim carrying crossbar (*patibulum*) to site of upright post (*stipes*). Center: low *tau* cross (*crux commissa*), commonly used by Romans at time of Christ. Upper right: rendition of the *titulus* for Jesus, with name and crime—Jesus of Nazareth, King of the Jews—written in Hebrew, Latin, and Greek. Lower right: possible methods of attaching titles to *tau* cross (left) and Latin cross (right).

Taken from William D. Edwards, Wesley J. Gabel, and Floyd E. Hosmer, "On the Physical Death of Jesus Christ," *Journal of the American Medical Association* 255 (1986): 1458. Used with permission of Mayo Foundation for Medical Education and Research.

---

[21] Ibid., 1459.

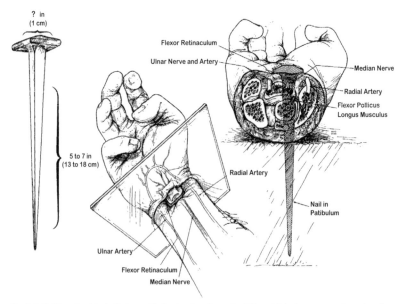

Fig. 3.3: *Nailing of wrists.* Left: iron nail. Center: location of nail in wrist, between carpals and radius. Right: cross section of wrist, at level of plane indicated at left, showing path of nail, with probable transection of median nerve and impalement of *flexor pollicis longus*, but without injury to major arterial trunks and without fractures of bones.

Taken from William D. Edwards, Wesley J. Gabel, and Floyd E. Hosmer, "On the Physical Death of Jesus Christ," *Journal of the American Medical Association* 255 (1986): 1459. Used with permission of Mayo Foundation for Medical Education and Research.

While our contemporary definition of "hand" clearly separates it from the wrist, the Greek word used for "hand" in the New Testament includes the wrist as part of the hand.[22] As such, the nails securing Jesus's hands to the *patibulum* could have pierced the wrists and this still would have been perfectly compatible with an accepted definition of "hand." In determining what part of the hand would be tough enough to support a hanging body, it is generally agreed by most authorities that the part of the palm closest to the fingers does not have enough tissue bulk to resist tearing when body weight is applied. Further, any nail traversing this part of the hand would quite likely

---

[22] Gerhard Kittel and Gerhard Friedrich, *Theological Dictionary of the New Testament*, trans. Geoffrey W. Bromiley, 10 vols. (Grand Rapids, MI: Eerdmans, 1974), 9:424. The Greek word *cheir*, commonly translated "hand" in English, was understood to mean the wrist and hand together. A passage where this word is used for "hand" is John 20:24–29.

fracture one of the hand bones. In contrast, any nail entering the upper hand adjacent to the muscle mass at the base of the thumb would be at a satisfactory entrance point to support a hanging body without this adverse tearing effect. Zugibe has argued that this was probably where the nail was placed.[23] He has further noted that if the nail was angled at about 15 degrees to exit at the level of the wrist, no hand bones would be broken. A second option is that proposed by Edwards and his colleagues from the Mayo Clinic. They contend that a nail placed in the wrist between the two forearm bones where they articulate with the bones of the upper hand would also spare any bone fracture and allow the support of a hanging body[24] (see figure 3.3).

Which option actually occurred will probably never be known. If the paintings depicting Jesus's crucifixion in the early centuries following his death, in which the nails are shown to enter the hand in the region of the upper palm, are any indication of what was passed on by tradition, then Zugibe's proposal is more likely. Irrespective of this uncertainty, one thing that is certain is that the median nerve was severely traumatized by the nailing, regardless of which approach was used (see figure 3.3). The median nerve serves two important functions. One is sensory, meaning that it allows sensations such as touch, temperature, and pain to be perceived from the skin enveloping most of the thumb and index and middle fingers and to a lesser extent some of the ring finger. The other is motor, meaning that it provides innervation to the thumb and index finger to enable them to perform flexion movements. Such innervation also enables the thumb to oppose itself to the other fingers of the hand so that a gripping function can be carried out.

Without doubt, both functions were severely impaired as a result of nerve damage that occurred from the nailing. It is highly unlikely that Jesus would have had any gripping function in either hand, had he survived the crucifixion. More importantly, severe pain would have emanated from this nerve injury and would have plagued him until he ultimately died. Known today as causalgia, it was first described

---

[23] Zugibe, *Crucifixion of Jesus*, 78–79.
[24] Edwards et al., "On the Physical Death of Jesus Christ," 1459.

by the neurologist Silas Weir Mitchell during the American Civil War in patients sustaining nerve injuries, particularly those involving the hand and forearm.[25] Causalgia is typically characterized by severe burning and electrical-like shooting pains that manifest themselves near the site of the nerve injury and radiate outward.[26] Thus, in the case of Jesus, the pain would originate where the nail had traversed the median nerve and very likely would radiate toward the fingernails as well as the upper forearm. It is not unusual for this shooting pain to be accompanied by increased sweating, local tissue swelling, and muscle spasms. The skin may also demonstrate changes in temperature and color. This pain is usually continuous and may be triggered by emotional stress, local movement of the affected area, and even touch. It is not surprising, then, that individuals experiencing causalgia do everything in their power to keep the injured site as immobile as possible. Obviously this was not an option for Jesus, since his impaled hands would be constantly jarring as he hung on the cross. One cannot begin to imagine the awful pain that he must have experienced.

Once the nails had been placed in Jesus's hands, the *patibulum* and his attached body would be hoisted upward by the soldiers attending to him to anchor it to the top of the *stipes*. The *stipes* was the vertical portion of the cross that was usually anchored in the ground, thereby making it easier to use for repeated crucifixions rather than having to dig a new hole and secure it in place each time.[27] Although we usually think of the cross as resembling in form what most of our jewelry crosses look like, the actual form upon securing the *patibulum* to the *stipes* was probably more like a "T" (Greek *tau*). Again, the pain that Jesus must have experienced during the attachment of these two pieces of the cross would have been unbearable.

Jesus's feet were next nailed to the *stipes* (see figure 3.4). As with the impalement of the hands, precisely how this was accomplished remains unknown. Some scholars believe that one foot was placed on

---

[25] S. W. Mitchell, G. R. Morehouse, and W. W. Keene, *Gunshot Wounds and Other Injuries of Nerves* (Philadelphia: J. B. Lippincott, 1864), 164.
[26] W. Russell Brain and J. N. Walton, "Causalgia," in *Brain's Diseases of the Nervous System* (London: Oxford University Press, 1968), 767–768.
[27] Zugibe, *Crucifixion of Jesus*, 46.

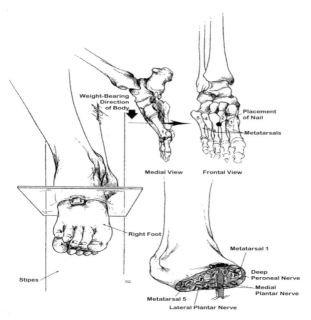

Fig. 3.4: *Nailing of feet.* Left: position of feet atop one another and against *stipes*. Upper right: location of nail in second intermetatarsal space. Lower right: cross section of foot, at plane indicated at left, showing path of nail.

Taken from William D. Edwards, Wesley J. Gabel, and Floyd E. Hosmer, "On the Physical Death of Jesus Christ," *Journal of the American Medical Association* 255 (1986): 1460. Used with permission of Mayo Foundation for Medical Education and Research.

top of the other, using a single nail.[28] (Figure 3.4 assumes this theory.) Others believe that each foot was nailed separately.[29] Those who accept this latter approach have also suggested various possibilities by which this could occur. These have ranged from each foot being nailed to opposite sides of the *stipes*, to both feet being placed next to each other on the front part of the *stipes* with the nails traversing the upper foot to exit at the level of the ankle (with the toes dangling freely), or with a nail being driven through each mid foot so that the sides of the feet are flush with the *stipes*, forcing the knees to be slightly bent. Zugibe argues that this last possibility would be less likely to fracture any foot bones (since no bones were broken in Jesus's body) and

---

[28] Edwards et al., "On the Physical Death of Jesus Christ," 1460–1461.
[29] Zugibe, *Crucifixion of Jesus*, 93–97.

because the soles of the foot could more easily be held flush with the *stipes* by one of the soldiers while another was driving the nail into the cross.[30] While the logic of this argument is compelling, we will never really know which option actually occurred.

As with the severe pain experienced by Jesus from the nailing of his hands to the *patibulum*, excruciating pain would also result from the spikes being driven through his feet. If the Zugibe proposal for the impalement of Jesus's feet is correct, then branches of the medial plantar nerves would be injured, eliciting a causalgia-like pain response similar to that in his hands. Even if some other nailing approach had been employed, there is no doubt that horrendous pain would be evoked. Thus, any movement of the feet, no matter how minimal, would trigger the pain. More importantly, any attempt that Jesus would undertake to move his legs, to alleviate the bending of his knees, or to overcome cramping would trigger unbearable pain in both his feet and hands. This pain would continue unrelentingly throughout his time on the cross.

After the nailing was completed, the gruesome process of dying began. It must be remembered that a Roman crucifixion existed for one purpose: to consummate the death of its victim in the most brutal way, no matter how long this might take. Survival was not an option. For some victims, death occurred in a matter of hours, while for others the process extended for days. There are reports of crucified people hanging on crosses for as long as three to four days in a semi-alive state and having their dying flesh become prey for vultures.[31] The duration of the suffering was greatly influenced by the physical state of the victim at the time of the nailing. If severe flogging had occurred prior to crucifixion, the duration of life after nailing was often short. In the case of Jesus, he lived at most only six hours.

So what did Jesus experience on the cross, and what ultimately brought about his death? As previously emphasized, the nerve injuries induced by the nails were responsible for excruciating pain from the resultant causalgia, unlike anything that you or I can compre-

---

[30] Ibid.
[31] Edwards et al., "On the Physical Death of Jesus Christ," 1461.

hend. Every movement, no matter how minor, triggered paroxysms of pain. Further, changes in temperature, sunlight, and even breezes were additional triggering mechanisms. Keep in mind as well the scalp pain elicited by the crown of thorns, not to mention the raw skin and exposed muscle resulting from the flogging that would have activated a whole separate array of pain from rubbing against the splintered wood of the cross. As if the gruesomeness of these images is not enough, remember also the shock-like state to which his body was subjected from the blood and body fluid losses induced by the flogging and the severe state of exhaustion from lack of sleep or rest from the time of his arrest.

The role of asphyxiation in contributing to Jesus's death has been debated over the years by those interested in the medical aspects of his crucifixion. This debate has ranged from its playing a major role[32] to that of playing little to no role.[33] Having taken care of hundreds, if not thousands, of critically ill patients, I believe that asphyxiation was a significant contributing factor. As a basic definition, asphyxiation simply means inadequate oxygen availability to body tissues because of disturbed lung function, resulting ultimately in multiple organ dysfunction, unconsciousness, and death.

I base this contention on at least three considerations. The first is the significant blood loss induced by the flogging. While the extent of this loss will never be known, it clearly was substantial enough to create a life-threatening situation independent of the subsequent effects of the crucifixion. One consequence of this hemorrhage is the decrease in the oxygen carrying capacity of the remaining circulating blood in Jesus's body, because of the resulting decrease in the amount of hemoglobin. Hemoglobin is the substance in the red blood cell component of blood that picks up oxygen in the lungs from inhaled air and carries it to the tissues of the body so that it can be used for their important metabolic processes. Due to this deficiency, all tissues of Jesus's body became severely compromised in carrying out their essential functions. The only way this situation could be reversed would be through

---

[32] Ibid., 1461 and 1463.
[33] Zugibe, *Crucifixion of Jesus*, 101–122.

increasing the amount of oxygen inhaled (so that the hemoglobin available could transport the most oxygen possible) and by providing blood transfusions to replace the red blood cells (and thus more hemoglobin for oxygen transport). Since neither of these capabilities were available in the first century (actually not available until the twentieth century), and would not have been provided to Jesus anyway, because he was on "death row," his shock-like state would have continued throughout his crucifixion.

Once the crucifixion commenced, the second consideration would come into play, namely, the severe pain from the nailing of his hands and feet. Thus, every time he took a breath, the movement and tension of his impaled body would exacerbate this excruciating pain, not only in each extremity but also in his raw back when it rubbed against the vertical *stipes*, the latter motion also inducing further blood loss (and thereby a continued loss of hemoglobin). The normal response of humans when experiencing pain is to do everything we can to lessen its magnitude. While modern medicine seeks to accomplish this goal with painkillers, this luxury was also not available to Jesus. Thus, the only way he could lessen his own pain would be through decreasing the frequency of breathing and the intensity of its magnitude. The net result of these actions is more shallow breathing that then further impairs the oxygen uptake by hemoglobin and its distribution to the rest of the body. Add to these observations the third consideration of pure exhaustion. The lack of sleep throughout the night of his interrogations and trials as well as the horrendous emotional stress and physical abuse associated with these events would have created a state of incredible exhaustion which, when added to the tormenting pain and decreased hemoglobin in his blood, made any chance of effective breathing and adequate tissue oxygenation virtually impossible over any extended period of time. In commenting on these physical derangements, Edwards and colleagues offer these important observations:

> The major pathophysiologic effect of crucifixion, beyond the excruciating pain, was a marked interference with normal respiration, particularly exhalation. The weight of the body, pulling down on the

outstretched arms and shoulders, would tend to fix the intercostal muscles in an inhalation state and thereby hinder passive exhalation. Accordingly, exhalation was primarily diaphragmatic, and breathing was shallow. It is likely that this form of respiration would not suffice and that hypercarbia would soon result. The onset of muscle cramps or titanic contractions, due to fatigue and hypercarbia, would hinder respiration even further.[34]

The "hypercarbia" referred to in this comment is the buildup of carbon dioxide in the blood because it is not adequately breathed out during exhalation due to the impaired respiration. As this retained carbon dioxide increases in concentration over time, it can elicit any number of effects on the central nervous system including apprehension, confusion, coma, and eventually death. Carbon dioxide retention also induces a state of acidosis in the blood, which along with the impaired oxygen levels results in rhythm disturbances in the heart (ineffective beating) that commonly lead to cardiac arrest if not reversed.[35] The only way these dire circumstances could have any chance of being effectively treated would be for a person as severely traumatized as Jesus to be given the benefits of modern critical care management, which would include placing him on a breathing machine, delivering copious amounts of oxygen, and restoring the blood that had been lost with multiple blood transfusions. Even with such sophisticated care, survival could by no means be guaranteed and would involve a long process, extending over many weeks, to also deal with the extensive wounds. Obviously, such care did not exist in the first century and certainly would not have been available to Jesus even if it had existed.

It should be clear from the foregoing discussion that the brutalized body of Jesus was on a trajectory to a fatal outcome. It was simply a matter of time until death would overtake him. If one reconstructs the biblical accounts from the time the flogging was completed (around 9 a.m.) until he actually died (about 3 p.m.), the maximum amount

---

[34] Edwards et al., "On the Physical Death of Jesus Christ," 1461.
[35] Philip S. Barie and G. Tom Shires, "Hypercarbia," in *Surgical Intensive Care* (Boston: Little, Brown, 1993), 288–289.

of time on the cross was about 6 hours and in actuality was probably much less. So what caused Jesus's death? In my judgment the most likely explanation was cardiorespiratory arrest from a fatal cardiac arrhythmia, which simply means that the heart and lungs failed to function any longer due to inadequate oxygenation, hypercarbia, and the associated acidosis. I have seen this combination of factors frequently elicit a fatal arrhythmia such as ventricular fibrillation, which, if not quickly reversed, will result in sudden death. Thus, death was the inevitable outcome for Jesus (see figure 3.5).

Since the Jewish Sabbath was to begin the evening of the same day that Jesus was crucified, the Jews were anxious that he would die prior to its commencement so that his burial could also be completed. A common means of hastening death was to break the victim's legs and thereby accelerate asphyxiation. Thus, Pilate was asked for permission that this procedure might be performed on Jesus (see John 19:31–37). To his surprise, he learned that Jesus was already dead (see Mark 15:44–45). This wonderment exhibited by Pilate does not mean, as some have speculated, that Jesus was simply in an unconscious state; rather, it attests to the moribund condition that Jesus was in when hung on the cross and that he died more quickly because of it than was usually the case in crucifixions. Being satisfied that Jesus was indeed dead, there was no reason for Pilate to order the breaking of his legs. Accordingly, Pilate was willing to give the body to Joseph of Arimathea (see next chapter) for burial. Prior to removing the body from the cross, one of the soldiers guarding Jesus thrust a spear into his side, from which flowed blood and water. Precisely why this additional act of brutality was inflicted will never be known. The likely explanation is to ensure that Jesus really was dead and thereby to alleviate once and for all any lingering doubt about this outcome. Another possibility is that it was just a malicious manifestation of the hatred of his captors.

The significance of the blood and water from the wound inflicted by the spear has been the subject of considerable speculation. The fact that eleven different hypotheses have been put forward to explain this

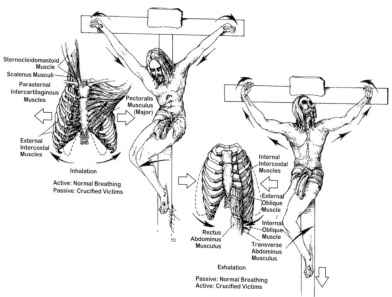

Fig. 3.5: *Respirations during crucifixion.* Left: inhalation. With elbows extended and shoulders abducted, respiratory muscles of inhalation are passively stretched and thorax is expanded. Right: exhalation. With elbows flexed and adducted and with weight of body on nailed feet, exhalation is accomplished as active, rather than passive, process. Breaking legs below knee would place burden of exhalation on shoulder and arm muscles alone and soon would result in exhaustion asphyxia.

Taken from William D. Edwards, Wesley J. Gabel, and Floyd E. Hosmer, "On the Physical Death of Jesus Christ," *Journal of the American Medical Association* 255 (1986): 1461. Used with permission of Mayo Foundation for Medical Education and Research.

occurrence[36] suggests that no consensus will ever be reached. Of additional note, the side of the chest in which the wound occurred was never designated by the Gospel in which it was described (see John 19:31–38). Despite this latter uncertainty, tradition has depicted this wound as being on the right side. If this is correct, the explanation by Zugibe[37] concerning the blood and water is the most compelling of the possibilities proposed. He offers the following sequence to explain these findings:

> The most plausible hypothesis . . . is . . . that the spear pierced the right atrium of the heart (right upper chamber), which would have been filled

---

[36] Zugibe, *Crucifixion of Jesus*, 141.
[37] Ibid., 139–140.

with blood because just prior to cardiac arrest, the heart contracts and ejects blood into circulation for the last time. In response, the right atrium fills up passively with blood because of this increased pressure through the circulation. A massive pleural effusion (fluid around the lungs) that had slowly accumulated in the hours following the brutal scourging (pleural effusion is commonly seen a few hours following beatings about the chest) was already present. The sudden thrust of the spear into the chest by one of the soldiers penetrated the pericardium and right atrium. The quick, jerking motion used to pull out the spear then carried the blood that had adhered to the blade and some of the pleural effusion from the pleural cavity, resulting in the phenomenon of "blood and water." However, there would not be any watery fluid extruding from the chest because after the spear was withdrawn, air would rush into the chest, creating increased pressure in the chest cavity causing a pneumothorax (collapse of the lung). The only watery fluid and blood flowing out of the wound would be due to the initial penetration by the lance (immediately prior to collapse) and small amounts of blood from the right atrium of the heart carried out of the wound on the spear tip. This would cause the fluid level around the lung to drop because there would be more space in the chest due to the collapsed lungs. If the *crucarius* [i.e. Jesus, the crucified victim] was not already dead at the time of the spear thrust, there would be no chance for survival because the punctured heart would pump blood into the chest cavity.[38]

Could Jesus Have Survived the Crucifixion?

Those who espouse the swoon theory as an explanation for Jesus's death often cite a passage from the writings of Josephus in which a person allegedly survived a crucifixion. It is argued that this episode proves that crucifixion is a survivable event and thus Jesus could have also survived this form of execution. In fact, in Schonfield's book *The Passover Plot*, which we have discussed, the Josephus passage is referred to multiple times and used to validate the idea that Jesus planned his own death and would have been alive when removed from the cross if the spear had not been thrust into his side. So what does the passage say? Although brief, the passage in question reads as follows:

> I saw many captives crucified, and remembered three of them as my former acquaintance. I was very sorry at this in my mind, and went

---

[38] Ibid., 140.

with tears in my eyes to Titus, and told him of them; so he immediately commanded them to be taken down, and to have the greatest care taken of them, in order to their recovery. Yet two of them died under the physician's hands, while the third recovered.[39]

Unfortunately, no additional information is provided. We know nothing about the details of those crucifixions, including the length of time that had elapsed before these individuals were removed from the cross, whether they had been flogged ahead of time, and how they were secured to the cross. While most victims were nailed to the cross as Jesus was, some were secured with ropes around their wrists and ankles. If this latter approach had been used, the magnitude of pain would be much less than with impalement with spikes and the corresponding emotional and physical stress on the body would be equally less. Further, even though two of Josephus's friends died, we know nothing about the one who supposedly lived. Did he live a normal life, or did the ravages of crucifixion eventually shorten his survival? Thus, comparing his situation with that of Jesus's crucifixion is pure conjecture and speculation. Regardless of this Josephus passage, anyone who thinks that Jesus was alive when removed from the cross, irrespective of whether the spear had been thrust into his side, really has no understanding of the brutality he went through and the effects on his body that are simply incompatible with survival. The swoon theory, then, should be forever buried, as it has no rational basis to explain Jesus's condition when declared dead.

Conclusion

So, could Jesus have survived the crucifixion? Based on what we know about this method of execution and the biblical account of his death, the answer to this question is an unequivocal no. Accordingly, when Jesus was taken down from the cross, he had indeed died. As such, when discussing his alleged resurrection, the issue is not whether he was resuscitated from some swoon-like state in the cool, moist air in the tomb where he was placed, but whether he actually did rise from the dead.

---

[39] Josephus, *Life of Flavius Josephus* 420–421.

4

WHAT'S SO IMPORTANT ABOUT AN EMPTY TOMB AND UNDISTURBED GRAVE CLOTHES?

If Jesus truly did rise from the dead, two forms of evidence are absolutely mandatory, irrespective of whether any other documentation can be provided. The first is an empty tomb. If he really died, as we saw compellingly in the last chapter, then the tomb where he was buried must no longer contain his corpse. While an empty burial site by itself does not prove a resurrection, it is absolutely crucial for its validation. Similarly, there must be witnesses who knew him prior to his death who can attest to the fact that he was indeed alive after supposedly rising from the dead. Only if the burial site is empty, though, is the testimony of such witnesses credible; otherwise anyone walking around claiming to be the resurrected Jesus is an imposter, no matter how much he may act and look like him. Since Christianity has alleged for the past two thousand years that both pieces of evidence are valid, how foolproof are they? This chapter will examine the arguments for the empty tomb, while the next will consider the testimony of those who presumably saw Jesus post-resurrection.

Christ's Entombment

All four Gospels are in agreement that Jesus died, was buried, and rose again from the dead. Each Gospel likewise asserts that Jesus was buried in a private tomb hewn out of a rock, belonging to Joseph of Arimathea. Although we have limited biographical information about him, we do know that Joseph was a rich man (Matt. 27:57), a respected member of the Sanhedrin (i.e., council) (Mark 15:43; Luke 23:50), a follower of Jesus, albeit secretly (Matt. 27:57; John 19:38), and a good and righteous person who did not agree with the decision to crucify Jesus (Luke 23:50–51). While various critics over the years have suggested that Joseph was a fictitious character and that the "tomb story" regarding his involvement in Jesus's burial has no credibility, there is not a shred of evidence supporting such allegations. Even if all other Gospel sources for his historicity were missing, the fact that Luke's Gospel validates his existence should suffice. As noted in chapter 2, Luke was considered a very meticulous historian, with scholars attesting to the accuracy and trustworthiness of both the Gospel that bears his name and his book of Acts.

The observation that a man of Joseph's stature personally attended to the details of Christ's burial and entombment lends additional credence to the discussion in the last chapter about Jesus being truly dead when taken down from the cross. A man like Joseph would have had nothing to gain and everything to lose if he had purported that Jesus was dead when in reality he was not. We are also informed in John's Gospel (John 19:38–42) that Nicodemus, the man who earlier had visited Jesus at night (see John 3), participated in the burial preparations, bringing a mixture of myrrh and aloes to anoint the burial clothes. Finally, when the body of Jesus was actually placed in the tomb, Mary Magdalene and Mary the mother of Joses saw where the body was laid (see Matt. 27:61; Mark 15:47; Luke 23:55). Thus, four witnesses could attest to the certainty of Jesus being dead and then being placed in a tomb.

These burial specifics become especially important in dealing with the issue of the empty tomb. The notion put forward by some individuals (who deny any possibility of a resurrection) that the followers of Jesus did not know where he was buried and mistakenly assumed that he had risen from the dead, because they visited the wrong burial site, flies in the face of common sense and reason. If Joseph of Arimathea was responsible for Jesus's burial and was assisted in this effort by Nicodemus, with the two Marys watching, at least these four people knew exactly where Jesus was entombed. Further, the Gospels give multiple examples of how close-knit the followers of Jesus were as a group. Consequently, it is not inconceivable that most if not all of the serious followers of Christ knew the location of the burial site. To speculate that the report of an empty tomb was simply a result of the disciples visiting the wrong tomb has no logical basis in fact.

How then is the empty tomb to be explained? Does an empty tomb necessarily mean a resurrection, or is some other explanation possible? Additionally, the Gospels of both Luke and John tell us that the grave clothes were still present in the empty tomb even though Jesus's body was missing (see Luke 24:12 and John 20:1–8). Of what importance is this? These questions form the basis of our continuing discussion.

Why Was the Tomb Empty?

Regardless of one's personal perspective on the resurrection, a careful and objective reading of the Gospels makes it abundantly clear that each writer firmly believed that Jesus rose from the dead, and each writer linked the empty tomb to this event as an important corroborating piece of evidence. Little wonder, then, that those who argue that the resurrection was a hoax have centered much effort in attempting to refute the "empty tomb story." Despite twenty centuries of efforts to disprove the empty tomb, virtually no convincing alternative explanations have been proposed.

So how certain is the evidence for the empty tomb? You will ultimately have to decide, but as we review the arguments attempting to disprove it, keep asking yourself how compelling these challenges really are. I think you will be surprised to see that most of them are exceedingly weak. In discussing these challenges, they generally can be categorized under two broad headings: 1) efforts to explain away the significance of the empty tomb, and 2) efforts to refute the idea that an empty tomb ever existed.

Efforts to Explain Away Its Significance

When attempting to challenge the significance of the empty tomb, four arguments have been commonly offered: (1) the disciples were mistaken concerning the actual burial site and went to the wrong tomb only to find it empty; (2) Jesus was not actually dead when placed in the tomb but was simply unconscious (the swoon theory), and when he revived he was able to escape; (3) the body was stolen; and (4) the female witnesses could not be trusted. But what evidence exists for any of these arguments? We have already considered the first challenge: it would be absurd to think that Joseph, Nicodemus, and the two Marys did not know where Jesus was buried, given that they were present when his body was placed in the tomb—and the disciples would have had easy access to this information through them. Further, the Jewish leadership had requested that a Roman guard be placed at the tomb of Jesus to prevent the disciples from stealing his body and thereby faking a resurrection (see Matt. 27:62–66). Thus, the location of Jesus's tomb was public knowledge, available to anyone wishing to visit the site. The "wrong tomb" theory, therefore, really has no credibility.

Before discussing the other possibilities, several features of Jesus's burial must be considered. The Gospels indicate that the tomb was "cut out of a rock." This is consistent with what we know about tombs in Palestine during the first century, especially those owned by rich people such as Joseph.[1] Accordingly, the tomb would be situated in the side of a hill with a walk-in entrance. We are further told that Joseph "rolled a great stone to the entrance of the tomb" after placing the body of Jesus in it (Matt. 27:59–60). Such stones were like massive circular wheels, made of limestone, and often weighed one to two tons.[2] To anchor them in place would frequently require the assistance of several able-bodied men. Once the stone was anchored, the corpse was secure within the tomb. Anyone desiring to remove the corpse would at the very least need to have the means of dislodging the stone blocking the entrance; obviously, this would present its own unique challenges. Of additional note, the body of Jesus was wrapped in multiple strips of linen interspersed with burial spices. We are told that Nicodemus brought seventy-five pounds of these spices to the

---

[1] Alfred Edersheim, *The Life and Times of Jesus the Messiah, Volume 2* (Grand Rapids, MI: Eerdmans, 1962), 318–319, 617.
[2] Josh McDowell, *Evidence for Christianity* (Nashville: Thomas Nelson, 2006), 283–285.

burial (John 19:38–42). While we have no way of knowing whether all this poundage was used, we can assume that most of it was. Thus the corpse, wrapped in these linens and spices, was probably quite heavy.

In the previous chapter we considered the brutality of the crucifixion. There was no question that Jesus was dead when removed from the cross. Pilate was convinced of this, or he would not have given the body to Joseph. Joseph, Nicodemus, and the two Marys were equally convinced, or they would not have prepared the body for burial and placed it in the tomb. To even entertain the possibility that Jesus was still alive and somehow revived and subsequently effected his own escape from the tomb is beyond rational comprehension from a medical perspective. I have taken care of some badly traumatized patients, but few have come even close to being as badly beaten as Jesus was. On the outside chance that he was alive when removed from the cross, any chance of survival would have required around-the-clock intensive care. Further, once Jesus was placed in the tomb, the weight on his chest of the spice-laden cloths would have greatly impaired any chance of even partial breathing. Remembering also (from the previous chapter) that Jesus's hand function would have been severely impaired and that walking would have been virtually impossible, how could he have disengaged himself from the grave clothes and then removed the 2,000–4,000 pound rock sealing the tomb's entrance and exited the tomb? And all of this without being seen! It is simply inconceivable, and there is absolutely no evidence to support such an explanation for the empty tomb.

Others have proposed that the tomb was empty because Christ's body was stolen. But who would have had any desire to steal the body of Jesus? The Romans certainly were not interested. After quibbling with the Jewish leadership over whether Jesus had done anything egregious enough to warrant death, Pilate finally acceded to their wishes and ordered the crucifixion. When Jesus's body was confirmed dead, Pilate gave it to Joseph to bury. Finally, when the Jewish leaders were concerned that the disciples of Jesus might steal his body from the tomb and then allege that he had been resurrected, they convinced Pilate to post a Roman guard at the tomb's entrance to prevent this from occurring (see Matt. 27:62–66). It would be totally illogical for the Romans to turn around and steal the body themselves, when they had been so committed to preventing this from happening. Similarly, it would be contradictory for the Jews to steal Jesus's body, when they had pressed for his execution in the first place and requested a Roman guard be posted at the tomb's entrance to ensure that the body would not be stolen. Finally, when the tomb turned out to be empty, the Jewish leaders circulated a rumor that the disciples had stolen the body, not knowing what else to do or how to explain this unanticipated event (see Matt. 28:11–15). It must not go unnoticed that, despite what you or I might think of the validity of the empty tomb, the Jewish leadership was *absolutely convinced* that Jesus's body was no longer in the tomb. They saw that the stone blocking its entrance had been dislodged and that Jesus's corpse was missing.

But were the disciples really guilty of stealing the body? What motive would they have? Put yourself in their position. Your friend and leader, with whom you had associated for three years, had been brutally executed and now lay dead in a Palestinian grave. Although Jesus had said that he would rise again, the truth of this promise had never sunk in; any chance that Jesus would come back to life was probably the furthest thought from the disciples' minds. The only thing they could think of now was the sorrow of the moment and the uncertainty of the future. What were they to do? Their master had been taken from them; things were truly bleak. Stealing Jesus's body would accomplish nothing. It made no sense then, and it makes no sense now.

If for some strange reason the disciples had wanted to steal the body of Jesus, the likelihood of successfully accomplishing that goal would have been virtually nil because of the Roman guard posted at the tomb's entrance. Obviously, the reason for posting the guard was to prevent such an action from occurring. The individual guards were very much aware of that responsibility and of the adverse personal consequences if they failed in their mission. McDowell points out that flawless attention to detail was expected of Roman guards assigned to such duty, and failure was punishable by death. Furthermore, the seal that had been affixed to the stone blocking the entrance to the tomb stood for the power and authority of the Roman empire. Breaking this seal, which the disciples would need to have done to remove the body, would have resulted in the automatic execution—probably by crucifixion in an upside-down posture—of those responsible.[3] Thus, it is highly unlikely that Christ's disciples would even have tried to steal his body.

One final but less common explanation sometimes proposed to discredit the historicity of the empty tomb is that the "women simply got it wrong." It is noteworthy that each Gospel writer introduces the story of the empty tomb with women being the key witnesses. In our contemporary society this would not be a problem, but in the first-century world, women were not considered credible witnesses and were not allowed to function in this capacity in a court of law. As such, the fact that women rather than men were the first witnesses is sometimes used to undermine the credibility of an empty tomb. N. T. Wright addresses this issue while quoting from Celsus, a second-century Greek philosopher and vocal critic of Christianity:

> We see the trouble they had [as witnesses] when we read Celsus, who a century later pours scorn on the resurrection by saying, "This faith is just based on the testimony of some hysterical women."[4]

Wright disagrees with Celsus and points out the significance of this female witness to the resurrection from a historian's perspective:

> So it's fascinating that in Matthew, Mark, Luke, and John we have Mary Magdalene, the other Marys, and the other women. And Mary Magdalene, of all people (we know she had a very checkered career in the past), is chosen as the prime witness: there she is in all four accounts. As historians we are obliged to comment that if these stories had been made up five years later, let alone thirty, forty, or fifty years later, they would never have had Mary Magdalene in this role. To put

---

[3] Ibid., 285–293. McDowell provides a very useful and comprehensive discussion of Roman guards and their responsibilities as well as the purpose of a Roman seal and the consequences if such a seal were broken.

[4] N. T. Wright, "Appendix B: What Evidence Is There for the Resurrection of Christ?" In Anthony Flew, *There Is a God: How the World's Most Notorious Atheist Changed His Mind* (New York: HarperCollins, 2007), 207 (I am grateful to N. T. Wright for permission to use this quote).

Mary there is, from the point of view of Christian apologists wanting to explain to a skeptical audience that Jesus really did rise from the dead, like shooting themselves in the foot. *The early Christians would never, never have made this up.* The stories—of the women finding an empty tomb and then meeting the risen Jesus—must be regarded as solidly historical.[5]

Thus, far from undermining the evidence for an empty tomb, the witness of the women strongly supports its historical validity. It is as if the Gospel writers were saying, "As strange as it may seem, this is what actually happened, and women were the first to witness it."

Efforts to Refute Its Very Existence

In addition to the arguments just discussed that have been offered to explain the empty tomb, a number of unique challenges have surfaced in recent years. Each of these challenges hinges on the notion that there never was an empty tomb. I say these challenges are "unique" because incredible fanfare has accompanied them despite there being almost no solid evidence to support them. Three in particular deserve comment because they have been given much media attention, as though they were firmly accepted by contemporary New Testament scholarship, even though quite the opposite is true.

The first is the notion that Jesus wasn't buried at all, as the Gospel accounts allege, but that his body was tossed into some common grave along with other victims of crucifixion, to decompose and never be seen again. Any discussion then of an empty tomb would therefore be irrelevant. Proponents of this argument, popularized by John Dominic Crossan[6] of the Jesus Seminar and by the Episcopalian Bishop John Shelby Spong,[7] contend that, because of the egregious nature of their crimes, it was commonplace throughout the Roman empire during

---

[5] Ibid. (I am grateful to N. T. Wright for permission to use this quote). For further discussion of this issue by Wright, see his book *The Resurrection of the Son of God* (Minneapolis: Fortress, 2003), 607–608.

[6] J. D. Crossan, *Who Killed Jesus? Exposing the Roots of Ant-Semitism in the Gospel Story of the Death of Jesus* (San Francisco: HarperCollins, 1995), 160–188; Crossan's ideas are further developed in: J. D. Crossan and J. L. Reed, *Excavating Jesus: Beneath the Stones, Behind the Texts* (San Francisco: HarperCollins, 2001), 230–270.

[7] John Shelby Spong, *Resurrection: Myth or Reality?* (San Francisco: HarperSan Francisco, 1995), 241.

the first century for those executed by crucifixion not to be allowed private burials. As such, the Gospel stories purporting that Jesus was buried in Joseph's tomb are nothing more than myth.

Is there any truth in this theory? While it is true that many victims of crucifixion in Roman times were left hanging on their crosses to be eaten by the birds, or were tossed into a shallow grave to have their corpses ravaged by animals,[8] this did not appear to be the practice with the Jews in Roman-occupied Palestine during the time of Jesus. In a comprehensive review of Roman interactions with the Jewish people during this era in ancient history, New Testament scholar Craig A. Evans found that leaving the bodies of executed Jews unburied was clearly the exception rather than the rule.[9] In fact, Jewish burial customs were nearly always respected by the Romans. Not only were these sensitivities detailed in various Roman ordinances but they were also articulated in the writings of Josephus and Philo, two important historians of that era. Thus, Evans concludes that the Gospel accounts of Jesus's burial are indeed accurate, and he vigorously debates those who would argue otherwise.[10]

A second challenge concerns the so-called "Jesus Family Tomb." Discovered in Talpiot (a suburb of Jerusalem) in 1980, this tomb was found to contain nine burial bone boxes called ossuaries (a tenth one was supposedly stolen) on which were inscribed a number of names such as Yeshua bar Yoseph (Jesus son of Joseph), Marya (Mary), Mariamenou e Mara (thought to mean Mary or Miriam), Matya (short for Matthew), Yehuda bar Yeshua (Judah son of Jesus), and Yose (short for Joseph). Because these names were similar to those of the biblical Jesus and his family, various scholars have proposed that this was the tomb where Jesus and his family were buried. Film editor and journalist Simcha Jacobovici (who hosts the *Naked Archaeologist* on the History Channel) along with movie producer James Cameron

---

[8] Martin Hengel, *Crucifixion in the Ancient World and the Folly of the Message of the Cross* (Philadelphia: Fortress, 1977), 22–32.

[9] Craig A. Evans, *Jewish Burial Traditions and the Resurrection of Jesus* (http://www.craigaevans .com/Burial_Traditions.pdf), 1–13.

[10] Ibid., 11–13; similar arguments have been articulated by B. R. McCane, *Roll Back the Stone: Death and Burial in the World of Jesus* (Harrisburg, PA: Trinity Press International, 2003), 89–108.

(of *Titanic* fame) have made much of this discovery, and they produced a television documentary for the Discovery Channel in 2007 claiming that this was indeed very likely "The Lost Tomb of Jesus." Further, a book by Jacobovici and Charles R. Pellegrino (with a foreword by James Cameron) called "The Jesus Family Tomb" was also released in 2007 purporting the same conclusion.[11]

Obviously, if this is the tomb of Jesus, then any notion that the resurrection occurred is nothing more than a hoax. But how valid are the claims of Jacobovici and Cameron? Other than the names on the ossuaries, the evidence is far from compelling. While it is true that the names on these ossuaries bear a strong resemblance to names known to be members of Jesus's family, these names were very common in first-century Israel. To conclude that such names found in an ancient tomb in Palestine strongly indicates that this could be the Jesus family tomb is clearly stretching the point. More important are several other considerations. First, there is no evidence, either within the New Testament or in sources outside it, that Jesus was ever married; thus, it makes no sense to tie the inscription "Judah son of Jesus" to the Jesus of the Gospels. Further, the family of Jesus was from Nazareth (see Matt. 2:23; Luke 2:4, 39, 51; and John 1:45–46), not from Jerusalem; accordingly, it would hardly be likely that their family tomb would be in Jerusalem or its environs. Perhaps most telling is a symposium that was convened in January 2008 at Princeton Theological Seminary to discuss the Talpiot Tomb. Comprising the leading scholars in archaeology and other New Testament disciplines who had an interest in this issue,[12] the symposium reached the consensus opinion (ultimately articulated in writing) that this tomb was just "an ordinary middle-class Jerusalem burial cave" and that there was nothing unique about it that would suggest it belonged to Jesus and his family.[13] This being

---

[11] Simcha Jacobovici and Charles Pellegrino, *The Jesus Family Tomb: The Discovery, the Investigation, and the Evidence That Could Change History* (San Francisco: HarperSan Francisco, 2007).

[12] Duke University Religion Department, "The Talpiot Tomb Controversy Revisited" (http://duke religion.blogspot.com/2008/01/talpiot-tomb-contoversy-revisited.html). Excellent discussion of the Princeton Symposium and how the media tried to distort its conclusions.

[13] Thomas F. Madden, *Not Dead Yet: The Lost Tomb of Jesus One Year Later* (http://www.national review.com/articles/print/223979), March 21, 2008, 1–4.
See also Dillon Burroughs, *The Jesus Family Tomb Controversy: How the Evidence Falls Short* (Ann Arbor, MI: Nimble Books, 2007).

so, all the publicity by Jacobovici and his colleagues concerning the tomb's significance was clearly a gross overstatement that misled untold millions of people (more than 4 million people watched this documentary, not to mention those who read the book).

The third challenge derives from the apostle Paul's statement in 1 Corinthians 15:3–8, where he says,

> For I delivered to you as of first importance what I also received: that Christ died for our sins in accordance with the Scriptures, that he was buried, that he was raised on the third day in accordance with the Scriptures, and that he appeared to Cephas, then to the twelve. Then he appeared to more than five hundred brothers at one time, most of whom are still alive, though some have fallen asleep. Then he appeared to James, then to all the apostles. Last of all, as to one untimely born, he appeared also to me.

The fact that Paul makes no reference to Jesus being *entombed* has been interpreted by some to mean that Paul knew nothing about Jesus's actual burial site and thus was unaware of any claim that he was placed in Joseph's private tomb and then rose from the dead three days later. Accordingly, any references to an empty tomb in the Gospels, which were written many years later, were simply legends that had become popular over the years. Those holding this view contend also that any discussion of a resurrection by Paul was "spiritual" in nature rather than referring to reappearance in bodily form.[14] Proponents of this theory note that 1 Corinthians was probably written around AD 55–56, many years before any of the Gospels were written, allowing ample opportunity for myths and legends to develop regarding Jesus's resurrection.[15]

But is such reasoning tenable? The bulk of contemporary New Testament scholarship would answer with a resounding no. To surmise that Paul believed something because he failed to state things the way

---

[14] Gary R. Habermas, "Why I Believe the Miracles of Jesus Actually Happened," in *Why I Am a Christian*, ed. Norman L. Geisler and Paul K. Hoffman (Grand Rapids, MI: Baker, 2001), 119–124. This section contains an excellent discussion of Paul's view of the resurrection and challenges any notion that he did not believe in Jesus's burial and the subsequent empty tomb.

[15] See Norman Geisler, "The Dating of the New Testament," in *The Baker Encyclopedia of Christian Apologetics* (Grand Rapids, MI: Baker, 1999), 37–41.

one thinks they should have been stated is what is commonly called an "argument from silence." Anyone who works in science knows that silence is not adequate grounds on which to base a conclusion. When most people say that someone has died and is buried, the implication is that there is a specific burial site where the person is buried. The proposal that "buried" could refer to some common burial grounds where countless corpses are mixed together irrespective of whether the individuals occupying these bodies knew each other when alive is attempting to build a case on flimsy presupposition. To require that Paul specifically state that Jesus's body was placed in a tomb before conceding that he actually believed that this is precisely what happened is asking more than usual communication requires. In thinking of a close relative's death some years ago, I almost always limit my comments to the date she died and that she was buried in a particular town. I almost never specify the actual burial site, unless asked to do so. It seems logical that Paul would have spoken about Jesus in a similar way. N. T. Wright, in his book *The Resurrection of the Son of God*, concurs. He observes that the statement "buried, then raised" no more requires further clarification than a statement such as "I walked down the street" would require the qualifying words "on my feet."[16] Wright emphasizes that the burial of Jesus prior to his resurrection implies that he was entombed.

Paul also states in these verses that numerous people saw the risen Jesus some days after his death, and could be interviewed if there were any doubts about his having been raised. This whole line of thinking (death, burial, resurrection) makes sense only if the burial site where Jesus was placed was now empty and people had seen him in a post-resurrection body with their "own eyes." We will consider these post-resurrection appearances in detail in the next chapter.

Of additional note, the summary statement provided by Paul in these verses is thought to have been based on a creed that dates to within three to eight years following Jesus's crucifixion. The authenticity of this creed is attested by virtually all contemporary New

---

[16] N. T. Wright, *The Resurrection of the Son of God* (Minneapolis: Fortress, 2003), 321.

Testament scholars.[17] Paul's utterance of this creed is compatible with the conclusion that he knew the details of Jesus's death, where he was buried, and the fact that his tomb was eventually empty, suggesting that he had risen from the dead, and that many witnesses could attest to this fact. To conclude, as some have done, that Paul knew nothing about these details has no basis in fact. Paul went to Jerusalem within three years of Jesus's death to discuss matters with Peter and James concerning his Christian ministry (see Acts 9:26–28; Gal. 1:18–24), and at that time he most certainly would have learned any information that he might have been unaware of regarding Jesus's death, burial, and resurrection, since these events formed the very basis of the Christian faith of the early church.

Finally, the book of Acts, being a historical summary of the activities of the early church, depicts Paul as being very much alive even up to the final chapter of the book. As most scholars believe that Paul's actual death was around the mid-60s AD, this means that Acts was written sometime before this date.[18] Since Luke, who wrote this book, also wrote the Gospel named after himself, this further means that Luke's Gospel was written prior to Acts, because this latter book was a follow-up to the initial Gospel account (see Luke 1:1–4 and Acts 1:1). Further, it is almost universally agreed among scholars that Mark was the earliest Gospel. Thus, the accounts of Luke, Mark, and probably Matthew (see chapter 2 for more discussion) were written sometime between the death of Jesus (i.e., AD 30–33) and the death of Paul (mid-60s AD). Such being the case, there was only a 30-year hiatus between these two deaths to allow room for myth or legend to arise, making the details in these Gospels entirely credible concerning Christ's death, burial, and resurrection.[19] If the Gospel accounts were inaccurate in any way, or were to any degree based on myth or legend, living witnesses to these events could easily have come forward and

---

[17] Ibid.; Gary R. Habermas, "Why I Believe the Miracles of Jesus Actually Happened"; see pages 117–124 regarding creeds and their impact on Paul's thinking; see also Pinchas Lapide, *The Resurrection of Jesus: A Jewish Perspective* (Minneapolis: Augsburg, 1983).

[18] Gary R. Habermas, "Why I Believe the New Testament Is Historically Reliable," in *Why I Am a Christian*, ed. Norman L. Geisler and Paul K. Hoffman (Grand Rapids, MI: Baker, 2001), 149–150.

[19] Ibid., 147–160.

corrected any misinformation. We have no record that any such challenges occurred. If they had, Paul could also have easily set the record straight. Since he did not, we have no reason to believe that the Gospel accounts were inaccurate. Thus, it is appropriate to conclude that Paul knew of the empty tomb whether or not he specifically said so in the 1 Corinthians 15 passage.

Why Were the Grave Clothes Undisturbed?

In addition to the Gospel accounts of the empty tomb, the Gospels of Luke and John include the further observation that the burial clothes in which Jesus's body had been wrapped were still present and neatly placed in the tomb despite the fact that the body was absent from them (see Luke 24:12 and John 20:1–8). How are we to explain this curious finding?

Before considering possible explanations, familiarity with Jewish burial customs at the time when Jesus died is appropriate. The late biblical scholar and pastor James Montgomery Boice discusses these customs in his commentary on the Gospel of John.[20] Referring to the earlier work of Henry Latham, who was an expert on Middle Eastern customs and detailed them in his book *The Risen Master* (published in 1901),[21] Boice notes that the common burial custom was to wrap the body and head with separate cloths. The body was wrapped in linen cloths to cover its entire anatomy except for the face, neck, and upper shoulders, which remained exposed. The top of the head was then covered with a twirled burial cloth that looked much like a turban. In the burial of Lazarus, separate head and body coverings were used (see John 11:44), confirming the observations of Latham and suggesting that Jesus would have been buried in a similar way.

Like the missing body, the undisturbed grave clothes lend additional evidence for a resurrection. It would make no sense to remove the body from its burial clothes prior to robbing it. Robberies are most successful when they are carried out with speed and secrecy.

---

[20] James Montgomery Boice, *The Gospel of John: An Expositional Commentary, Volume 5* (Grand Rapids, MI; Zondervan, 1979), 268–275.
[21] Ibid., 270–272. Boice discusses Latham's writings on Jewish Burials (see Henry Latham, *The Risen Master* [Cambridge: Deighton Bill, 1901], 36–54).

To remove the grave wrappings from the corpse prior to stealing it would have slowed the process considerably and probably would have caused considerable commotion. Finally, it must also be mentioned that myrrh, one of the spices placed within the burial garments, was known to have a gummy consistency resulting in a stickiness and close adherence between the grave clothes and the body; as such, their separation would be especially difficult.[22] Assuming that all these stumbling blocks had been overcome, the extracted burial clothes would in all probability have been tossed in a heap, rather than left lying neatly and undisturbed in the tomb, as the Gospels attest.

For these reasons, the most logical explanation for the undisturbed grave clothes is that a resurrection did in fact occur. John (referring to himself as "the other disciple") was convinced of this when he witnessed the burial garments firsthand. Not only did he consider this finding *supportive* evidence for a resurrection, he also found it to be *sufficient* evidence, for we are told in his Gospel that he "saw and believed" (John 20:8). In John's mind there was no other way to explain what he had seen. He knew without a doubt that he would ultimately see Jesus in bodily form, because the undisturbed clothes sealed once and for all that he had risen from the dead.

As we reflect on Jesus's empty tomb, we are left with an absent body and neatly positioned burial garments. It is as if the body had vaporized! What would we have observed if we had personally viewed the resurrection? Boice has provided a very helpful visual image that comes as close to anything that I could imagine:

> If we had been present in the tomb at the moment of the Resurrection, we would have noticed either that the body of Jesus would have seemed to have disappeared or else that it was changed into a resurrection body and passed through the grave clothes and out of the sealed tomb just as it was later to pass through closed doors.
>
> What would have happened then? The linen cloths would have subsided once the body was removed because of the weight of the spices that were in them, and they would have been lying undisturbed where the body of Jesus had been. The cloth which surrounded the

---

[22] McDowell, *Evidence for Christianity*, 281.

head, without the weight of spices, might well have retained its con-
cave shape and have lain by itself separated from the body cloths by the
space where the Lord's neck and shoulders had been.[23]

It really does appear that Jesus arose from the dead!

What Does It All Mean?

What do we conclude from this analysis of the empty tomb and the
undisturbed grave clothes? I am reminded of the time when I was a
postdoctoral research fellow in gastrointestinal physiology. I had the
privilege of working with a professor who was very practical in assessing experimental findings. When analyzing results of an experiment
and attempting to provide the most cogent understanding of what they
meant, he always encouraged me to "go with the best fit." He believed
that too many investigators tried to explain things esoterically and in
so doing often missed the obvious. They "looked for zebras when they
should have been looking for horses."

This sage advice is especially pertinent in dealing with the empty
tomb of Jesus. For some two thousand years multiple explanations have
been offered to account for this event only to fall far short in providing
"the best fit" as to what it means. John picked up on the obvious as
soon as he beheld the empty tomb and the undisturbed grave clothes.
The "best fit" for him was that a resurrection had truly happened! Is
that *sufficient* evidence? For John it was. For most of us, probably not.
We would like additional evidence that a living body exists and can
be confirmed as belonging to the once-dead Jesus. Nonetheless, don't
miss the obvious as regards the empty tomb. It is hard to explain the
empty tomb, and especially the retained grave clothes in its interior,
without concluding that a resurrection occurred.

---

[23] Boice, *Gospel of John*, 272.

5

ARE 500 WITNESSES ENOUGH?

The empty tomb and the undisturbed grave clothes provide strong evidence that Jesus did, in fact, rise from the dead. Indeed, as we have seen, for the apostle John it was sufficient evidence to convince him of the resurrection. But what about people in Jesus's day and people down through the ages who might find even such strong evidence insufficient? For such skeptics, we turn now to the testimony of witnesses (including John himself) who actually saw the resurrected Jesus face to face.

The Importance of Witnesses

Before addressing this issue specifically, it is appropriate to make some comments regarding the importance of witnesses in our everyday lives. Although not often thought of as such, every time we are asked to provide references, whether for a job application, a possible promotion, an effort to obtain credit, or for entrance into some academic institution, we are actually providing witnesses. These witnesses vouch for who we are, our character, and our capabilities germane to the situation. Witnesses become especially important if you are involved in an accident and there is some dispute as to whether you or the other person is at fault. Often the fault issue remains unresolved unless an objective witness comes forward and details what he or she says happened from their unbiased perspective. In a court trial, witnesses can frequently determine whether the ultimate decision is for the defense or the prosecution.

In all these instances, the number of witnesses involved is relatively few—no more than two or four in most circumstances. In the case of the resurrection, 500-plus witnesses were available and could testify in support of the event. We know this from 1 Corinthians 15:3–8:

> For I delivered to you as of first importance what I also received: that Christ died for our sins in accordance with the Scriptures, that he was buried, that he was raised on the third day in accordance with the Scriptures, and that he appeared to Cephas, then to the twelve. Then he appeared to more than five hundred brothers at one time, most of whom are still alive, though some have fallen asleep. Then he appeared to James, then to all the apostles. Last of all, as to one untimely born, he appeared also to me.

Not only is this magnitude of witnesses impressive, but Paul indicates that most of them were still living and could be interviewed if there were any doubt regarding their position on the validity of the resurrection.

To understand the importance of this body of witnesses, a look at the process of scientific experimentation should prove helpful, since scientists are essentially *witnessing* whether their hypotheses can be verified. Let us say that an experiment is set up to determine whether item A is converted to item B under a particular set of circumstances. If the experiment is conducted ten times and A becomes B five times, we conclude that there is a 50 percent chance (probability) that the conversion will happen. But because it did *not* happen five times, there is the equal probability that A will not become B. If this outcome were to occur, it is highly unlikely that the original hypothesis was correct. On the other hand, if A becomes B eight out of ten times, then the probability increases to 80 percent, with only a 20 percent chance that it will not happen, giving substantially more support to the hypothesis. If A becomes B ten out of ten times, not only is the hypothesis strongly supported, but one would be tempted to conclude that the probability of this happening is 100 percent. Actually, it is somewhat less than that since, if the experiment were to be performed an eleventh time, A might not convert to B. Thus, from a statistical standpoint the probability would be somewhere between 95 and 100 percent, but not actually 100 percent.[1] The only way we can get closer to 100 percent is to increase the number of times the experiment is conducted. Accordingly, if the experiment were conducted 50 times and A became B each time, the probability is still not 100 percent because it may not happen the 51st time, but it is clearly 99 percent plus. If the experiment were conducted 100 times and A became B each time, the probability is still not quite 100 percent because the 101st time the experiment is performed A may not become B, but now the probability is of the order of 99.99999 percent. If the experiment were conducted 500 times and A became B each time, the probability is now for all intents and purposes 100 percent. Even though, the next time the experiment is performed, A may not become B, it now becomes mathematically absurd to think that this would happen. Reproducibility (i.e., repeatability) is extremely important in validating a scientific hypothesis, and the more times it can be demonstrated, the more secure the hypothesis becomes.

Most scientific experiments are conducted with the intent of determining whether there is a 95 percent probability of something happening. Ten to twenty experiments are often considered sufficient to establish this level of probability. If such probability cannot be achieved with this number of experiments, it more than likely does not exist. To conduct 50–100 additional experiments, or even more, is usually unnecessary, too time-consuming, and not an appropriate use of resources.

I have taken the time to show how reproducibility increases certainty in order to emphasize the importance of the large number of witnesses attesting to the resurrection. Not only do we have the 500-plus witnesses that the apostle Paul refers to in his Corinthian letter, but there are multiple other groups and individuals to whom Jesus revealed himself after the resurrection, as recorded in the Gospels (see table 5.1).

---

[1] Many excellent resources are available that discuss the concept of statistical probability. I recommend two books: G. W. Snedecor and W. G Cochran, *Statistical Methods*, 7th ed. (Ames: Iowa State University Press, 1980); M. Bland, *An Introduction to Medical Statistics*, 2nd ed. (London: Oxford University Press, 1995). The reader is referred to this source material for a more comprehensive discussion of the statistical issues covered in this chapter.

TABLE 5.1: Post-resurrection Appearances of Jesus

Place	Witnesses	Type of Interaction	Biblical Reference
Empty tomb	Mary Magdalene	Saw, talked with, and touched* him	John 20:11–18
Empty tomb	Mary Magdalene and the other Mary	Saw, talked with, and touched him	Matt. 28:1–10
Emmaus road	Two individuals	Saw, talked with, and ate* with him	Luke 24:13–32
Unspecified place	Peter	Saw* and talked* with him	Luke 24:34; 1 Cor. 15:5
In a room (unspecified place)	Ten disciples (without Thomas)	Saw, talked with, touched* and ate with him	Luke 24:36–49; John 20:19–23
In a room (unspecified place)	Eleven disciples (including Thomas)	Saw, talked with, and touched* him	John 20:24–31
Along the Sea of Galilee	Seven disciples	Saw, talked with, and ate* with him	John 21:1–25
Unspecified place in Galilee	Eleven disciples	Saw and talked with him	Matt. 28:16–20; Mark 16:14–18
Unspecified place	500 individuals at once	Saw and talked* with him	1 Cor. 15:6
Unspecified place	James (Jesus's brother)	Saw and talked* with him	1 Cor. 15:7
Jerusalem	Eleven disciples	Saw and talked with him	Acts 1:3–8
Road to Damascus	Paul	Saw and talked with him	Acts 9:1–19; 1 Cor. 15:8

*Implied

The sheer volume of witnesses is staggering and places the burden of proof on those who would deny this event. It is not appropriate to say that these witnesses were self-deceived, hallucinating, or had seen a ghost or apparition rather than a real person. Even allowing for the unlikely possibility that some of these witnesses might have fallen into this category, it is not realistic to believe that this would have affected any appreciable number of them. Furthermore, most of the inner core of disciples who had been with Jesus during the three years of his earthly ministry interacted with him after his resurrection on at least four occasions. These included the two encounters in the locked room (John 20:19–31), the time when they went fishing with him (John 21), and the time of Christ's ascension (Acts 1:4–11). If Jesus was simply a ghost or a hallucination, these disciples might have been fooled once, but it is unreasonable to think that they could have been fooled four times in a row. Further, during the fishing expedition, they actually ate with him, indicating that he was a real person with a real body. Ghosts and apparitions do not eat. Finally, there is not a shred of evidence in the Gospel accounts or even in historical documents outside of Scripture that the person claiming to be the resurrected Jesus was a fraud. Likewise, in the book of Acts, which gives a historical review of the early rise of Christianity and its spread throughout the Roman empire, the reality of the resurrection is referred to countless times, with no credible challenge to its validity. Accordingly, we can conclude that the likelihood of the testimony of the 500-plus witnesses being wrong is so infinitesimally small as to render it beyond any reasonable doubt that the resurrection did in fact occur. As previously noted, if a scientific experiment were conducted 500 times and the result each time supported the hypothesis being tested, the odds of the hypothesis being wrong from a probability standpoint is so mathematically unlikely as not to be worth any serious consideration. Similar conclusions apply with respect to the 500-plus witnesses attesting to the resurrection.

But why couldn't the "resurrection story" have been just a myth neatly contrived by the disciples to explain the empty tomb? Wouldn't that also explain the Gospel accounts? And to prove such a myth, wouldn't you want plenty of witnesses? In his book *Loving God*, Charles Colson, the famed participant in the Watergate scandal who became a Christian through that experience, had these compelling observations regarding the myth theory:

> Even a cursory reading of the Gospels reveals not allegory or fable, but a straightforward narrative account. Moreover, Paul, an intimate associate of the original disciples, shatters the myth theory altogether when he argues that if Jesus was not *actually* resurrected, Christianity is a hoax, a sham. Nothing in Paul's writings remotely suggests mythology. . . .
>
> So if one is to assail the historicity of the Resurrection, . . . one must conclude that there was a conspiracy—a cover-up if you will—by eleven men with the complicity of up to five hundred others. To

subscribe to this argument, one must also be ready to believe that each disciple was willing to be ostracized by friends and family and live in daily fear of death, endure prisons, live penniless and hungry, sacrifice family, be tortured without mercy, and ultimately die—all without ever once renouncing that Jesus had risen from the dead!

In comparing this alleged resurrection conspiracy with the Watergate scandal, Colson comments further:

> This is why the Watergate experience is so instructive for me. If John Dean and the rest of us were so panic-stricken, not by the prospect of beatings and execution, but by political disgrace and a possible prison term, one can only speculate about the emotions of the disciples. Unlike the men in the White House, the disciples were powerless people, abandoned by their leader, homeless in a conquered land. Yet they clung tenaciously to their enormously offensive story that their leader had risen from His ignoble death and was alive—and was *the* Lord.
>
> The Watergate cover-up reveals, I think, the true nature of humanity. None of the memoirs suggest that anyone went to the prosecutor's office out of such noble notions as putting the Constitution above the President, or bringing rascals to justice, or even moral indignation. Instead, the writings of those involved are consistent recitations of the frailty of man. . . .
>
> Is it really likely, then, that a deliberate cover-up, a plot to perpetuate a lie about the Resurrection, could have survived the violent persecution of the apostles, the scrutiny of early church councils, the horrendous purge of the first-century believers who were cast by the thousands to the lions for refusing to renounce the Lordship of Christ? Is it not probable that at least one of the apostles would have renounced Christ before being beheaded or stoned? Is it not likely that some "smoking gun" document might have been produced exposing the "Passover plot"? Surely one of the conspirators would have made a deal with the authorities (government and Sanhedrin probably would have welcomed such a soul with open arms and pocketbooks!) . . .
>
> Take it from one who was inside the Watergate web looking out, who saw firsthand how vulnerable a cover-up is: Nothing less than a witness as awesome as the resurrected Christ could have caused those men to maintain to their dying whispers that Jesus is alive and Lord.[2]

---

[2] Charles W. Colson, *Loving God* (Grand Rapids, MI: Zondervan, 1983), 68–69.

If the resurrection truly was a myth and this great body of witnesses had orchestrated the myth and the subsequent perpetuation
thereof, all the Roman authorities and/or Jewish leadership would
have had to do to disprove it once and for all would be to produce the
corpse of the crucified Jesus. After all, they knew where he was buried
and had even placed a Roman guard at the tomb to prevent his body
from being stolen. Interestingly, two thousand years have elapsed and
we have no documentation that such a corpse was ever produced.

The Unique Witness of Thomas and James

The collective testimony of the 500-plus witnesses more than validates
the assertion that Jesus rose from the dead. In fact, as one observer
noted, "There is as much evidence for the Resurrection as there is for
any other event of that time, such as the assassination of Caesar or
the suicide of Cleopatra."[3] Thus, if one accepts the historicity of these
latter events, which to my knowledge has never been called into question by historians, the evidence for the resurrection on the basis of the
numbers of witnesses alone is overwhelming and cannot be dismissed
as irrelevant. And yet, even if we did not have all these witnesses, the
unique witness of two individuals has to be explained if the resurrection is still to be disputed. I am referring to Thomas, one of the
disciples of Jesus, and James, his brother.

Consider first the testimony of Thomas. For those with even a
casual familiarity with the Gospels, the name Thomas is well known.
He is frequently called "doubting Thomas" because he was not about
to accept any notion that Jesus had risen from the dead until he himself was able to analyze the evidence. I have a great deal of admira-
tion for Thomas. He was willing to admit his doubts and refrain from
drawing any conclusions until his inquiring mind was certain of the
evidence. He was acting as any credible scientist would, unwilling to
give his assent until he had fully evaluated the data.

So what was the issue bothering Thomas? As recorded in John
20:19–29, Jesus appeared before ten of the twelve disciples on the eve-

---

[3] C. Bernard Ruffin, *The Twelve: The Lives of the Apostles after Calvary* (Huntington, IN: Our Sunday Visitor, 1997), 123.

ning following his resurrection, validating that he had indeed risen from the dead. Judas obviously was not present, having committed suicide after betraying Jesus. Thomas was also absent, for reasons not stated. When the disciples who were present told Thomas that the risen Jesus had appeared to them, he refused to believe their report until he personally could view the nail prints in Jesus's hands and the site where the spear had pierced his side.

It is easy to criticize Thomas for his unbelief. Before doing this, however, put yourself "in his shoes." Thomas's friend Jesus had been brutally murdered by crucifixion, and his body had been placed in a tomb. To even entertain the possibility that Jesus might now be alive again went against all human logic. How could this dead man pull off his own resurrection? Had Thomas's fellow disciples really seen Jesus, or had they merely hoped against hope and imagined that he had risen from the dead? Little wonder, then, that Thomas wanted more compelling evidence and reassurance than just some fanciful words from colleagues who had been just as distraught as he, following Jesus's death.

Jesus reappeared to his disciples one week later, this time with Thomas present. Recognizing Thomas's disbelief, Jesus invited him to examine his wounds. Almost immediately it was clear to Thomas that this man standing in front of him was indeed the resurrected Jesus. Thomas's exclamation, "My Lord and my God!" (John 20:28) says it all. The evidence was sufficient, and any doubt had now been dissolved. By calling him "Lord," which was a common designation used for a teacher or master, Thomas recognized that the post-resurrection Jesus was the same Jesus he had known prior to his death. But he went even further and called him his "God." It is important that this affirmation not be missed. One must remember that Thomas was a practicing Jew and took the Ten Commandments (Ex. 20:1–17) very seriously. The first commandment stated that there was only one God and he was to be loved with one's entire being. The second stated that no substitutes were ever to be worshiped in place of this one God. Thus, for Thomas to call Jesus "my God" was acknowledging that the resurrected Jesus was more than just some man who had been raised from the dead; Thomas was affirming that this man was God himself in human flesh.

Thomas was never the same after this encounter. His whole life was radically changed. He was fully convinced that this person with whom he had associated for the previous three years was more than just a friend and teacher; he was indeed God in the flesh. To understand the lasting effect that this event had on Thomas, one need only track the course of his life from this point forward. In his excellent book *The Twelve*, C. Bernard Ruffin covers the activities of each of the disciples following the resurrection. In the chapter about Thomas, he provides compelling evidence that this disciple devoted the rest of his life to spreading the good news of Jesus's death and resurrection.[4] This evangelistic effort took him to Persia (which today would stretch from southern Turkey to Iraq and western Iran), Parthia (present-day northeastern Iran), and India. In fact, Thomas is generally credited with having brought Christianity to India. There is some evidence that Thomas also carried the gospel to China. Most of his later life, however, was spent in India, and numerous stories have been told about the risks he took to make the gospel known in that country. Most evidence suggests that he was martyred on July 3, AD 72, in the town of Mylapore in southern India.[5] The martyrdom presumably occurred at the hands of Hindu Brahman priests who were attempting to prevent the spread of Christianity. A tomb in Mylapore marks the site where Thomas is allegedly buried. Interestingly, Marco Polo referred to this tomb in one of his travel diaries as Thomas's burial site. Of further note, Marco Polo also recounts that, after having been fatally wounded with a spear, Thomas prayed while dying, "Lord, I thank Thee for all Thy mercies. Into Thy hands I commend my spirit."[6] Thus Thomas the "doubter" became a person of incredible faith because he was absolutely convinced that Jesus had conquered death.

The witness of James is equally noteworthy. His testimony is particularly telling because he was the biological brother of Jesus (Mary being the biological mother of both Jesus and James). While we have

---

[4] Ibid., 120–134.
[5] Ibid., 134. Mylapore today is part of the city of Chennai, previously known as Madras.
[6] J. M. Farquhar and G. Garitte, *The Apostle Thomas in India, According to the Acts of Thomas* (Kerala: Syrian Church Series, 1972) p. iv; Ruffin, *The Twelve*, 134.

very little detailed information about Jesus's family other than his father and mother, we do know that he had brothers and sisters (see Matt. 13:55–57; Mark 6:3), James being among them. We are also told that *none* of Jesus's brothers or sisters (which presumably includes James) believed in his being the Son of God prior to the resurrection (John 7:3–5; see also Matt. 12:46–50; Mark 3:21, 31–35). Consider what it would be like to have Jesus as a brother and then to learn later that he was God in the flesh. Whether you thought he was worthy of this designation would depend on what you thought of him and whether he had acted in a manner consistent with what you envisioned God to be like. At the very least I would suspect that you would expect fairness in his dealings with people, the absence of inappropriate emotional outbursts, impeccable honesty, a strong character, sensitivity to human need, a willingness to help those who are hurting, and genuine humility. In short, he would live his life in such a way that it was a constant and continual fulfillment of the Ten Commandments. We all know what we expect of others, and we are frequently disillusioned by not seeing these expectations realized. Any similar disillusionments regarding Jesus, if he were our brother, would quickly diminish the likelihood of our seeing him as anything special, let alone believing that he was God.

I have a brother, and although I respect and love him and consider him my friend, I am fully aware of his shortcomings. I have no doubt that if you were to ask him about me, he could list all of my imperfections and faults! Neither of us, even under the best of circumstances, would ever qualify for the designation of being God. And if either of us ever developed the illusion that we were God, an immediate psychiatric evaluation would be arranged!

The situation with Jesus was obviously different. Following his resurrection, he personally appeared to James (1 Cor. 15:7), and this appearance was enough to convince James that his brother was indeed God. Like Thomas, his life was radically changed thereafter. James's meeting with the risen Jesus was sufficient to change his attitude to him from one of opposition and hostility to one of complete loyalty and lifelong discipleship. The seriousness of this commitment is spelled out in the New Testament epistle authored by him, where he describes himself as "James, a servant of God and of the Lord Jesus Christ" (James 1:1). He later refers to Jesus as "our Lord Jesus Christ, the Lord of glory" (2:1).

That James so readily became Christ's disciple, post-resurrection, also shows that Jesus's life prior to the crucifixion had been totally consistent with what James thought God should be like. Nothing that James had observed in the life of his brother Jesus stood in the way of his believing that Jesus had now risen from the dead and that he was truly God.

So what happened to James after Jesus's resurrection appearance to him? While the details of that encounter are unknown, James's involvement in the rise of early Christianity is well described in the book of Acts. We first learn that he was a member of a faithful band of followers that had assembled in Jerusalem following Jesus's ascension (see Acts 1:14). We later find him in a leadership role in the Jerusalem church and presiding over the council of Jerusalem, when the decision was made to welcome Gentiles into the fellowship of the Christian church (see Acts 15). His assuming such a major role makes it obvious that James's commitment to spreading the gospel was indeed genuine.

We know from historical sources that James was the leader of the Jerusalem church for some thirty years, and that many Jews were converted to Christianity through his ministry.[7] This success was not without its consequences and ultimately resulted in James's death. The details of his martyrdom are summarized in the following account by Ruffin,[8] using historical material provided by the second-century historian Hegesippus:

> This happened in Jerusalem in the spring of A.D. 62, after the death of the incumbent governor Festus, and before the appointment of his successor. A number of the "ruling class" of the Jews had gone over to Christianity, and the high priest Ananias was enraged with homicidal fury. The Sanhedrin summoned James. Interestingly enough, they looked to him to restrain the Christians. All seventy-one members

---

[7] Ruffin, *The Twelve*, 71–87.
[8] Ibid., 84–86 (permission was granted by Our Sunday Visitor to use this quote).

of the council knew that there was no man in Jewry so zealous for the law as James. They also knew that he was at least sympathetic to Christianity. Moreover, they were aware that there had been friction between him and other Christian leaders over the observance of the law. Surely James did not go for this ridiculous monkey business that Jesus was the Messiah. They might be willing to concede that he was a great man. Their predecessors had killed Him, but, well, that was "just one of those things," a lamentable error in judgment. But the insistence that this Jesus was not just a good man but the Son of God Almighty and Israel's Messiah was intolerable. Surely, so devout a Jew as James could not believe this humbug. He could call together the leaders of the Christian community and tell them, "Let's get this straight: Jesus was a great man and it is good to reverence his ethical teachings like those of any other famous rabbi, but let's not say that he was God." This is what the Sanhedrin expected James to do. According to Hegesippus, they told James to "make the facts about Jesus clear to all who come for Passover day. We all accept what you say: we can vouch for it, and so can all the people, that you are a righteous man and take no one at his face value. So make it clear to the crowd that they must not go astray as regards Jesus: the whole people and all of us accept what you say. So take your stand on the temple parapet, so that from that height you may be easily seen and your words audible to the whole people." Thus, thirty years almost to the day after Jesus was crucified, James was to make a public speech declaring the "true facts" about Jesus Christ.

On Passover, the courts of the temple were crowded with thousands of worshipers as James prepared to speak before the greatest audience of his life and tell them the "true facts" about Jesus. He climbed, apparently, to a walkway above one of the colonnades, where he could be seen and heard easily. The worshipers packed themselves in an immense throng before him. In the crowd were members of the Sanhedrin. When the crowd grew silent upon seeing this man, respected by Jew and Christian alike, about to speak, several members of the Sanhedrin shouted up to James, "Righteous One, whose word we are all obliged to accept, the people are going astray after Jesus who was crucified; so tell us what is meant by the 'Door of Jesus.'"

The answer that James proclaimed to the throng below was not the one that the Sanhedrin anticipated. "Why do you question me about the Son of Man?" he shouted. "I tell you, He is sitting in heaven at the right hand of the Great Power and He will come on the clouds of heaven!"

The crowd broke into cheers of "Hosanna to the Son of David!" and the members of the Sanhedrin, insane with fury, decided there and then to kill James so as to intimidate the crowd and prevent further conversions. Several of them rushed to the top of the parapet where James was speaking and threw him off onto the pavement below, where he was surrounded by a mob of local toughs who had accompanied the city fathers. As James lay stunned on the ground, they began to stone him. James began to pray, "I beseech Thee, Lord God and Father, forgive them. They do not know what they are doing."

Some of the crowd in the temple courts were horrified and began to shout, "Stop! What are you doing? The Righteous One is praying for you!" But they were unable to rescue James because of the mob which surrounded him. Some of James's attackers became ashamed and withdrew, but one brazen fellow, armed with something like a sledgehammer, took it and brought it down on James's head, killing him instantly.

As should be obvious from the foregoing discussion, the witness of Thomas and James to the resurrection was not some casual affirmation. On the contrary, both of them were absolutely convinced that Jesus had risen from the dead and were willing to stake their lives on this conviction. Little could they have known that they would ultimately be martyred for this belief, but at no time did they ever deny the certainty in their minds that Jesus had in fact conquered death. For those who wish to gainsay the reality of the resurrection, the testimony of these two followers of Jesus and their willingness to place their lives in harm's way needs to be explained. People do not knowingly die in support of a myth.

So What Does the Evidence Show?

In this and the previous three chapters, we have considered six lines of evidence concerning the resurrection. These have included 1) the reliability of the New Testament (and especially the Gospels) as valid source material; 2) the certainty of Jesus's death; 3) the empty tomb; 4) the undisturbed grave clothes; 5) the volume of witnesses attesting to Jesus's appearances in bodily form; and 6) the willingness of witnesses to sacrifice their lives for their belief that the resurrection had occurred. In doing so, we have carefully reviewed the various explanations for these findings and have excluded those which rationally have no merit. Based on this analysis, the preponderance of evidence is overwhelmingly compelling for the conclusion that Jesus truly did conquer death and rise from the dead. You will have to decide whether you agree. But if, perchance, you do not find the evidence as compelling as I do, I think it is only fair to ask you why and to remind you that the burden of proof is yours.

In concluding this chapter, it is appropriate to reference Simon Greenleaf, the great legal scholar of the nineteenth century and Royall Professor of Law at Harvard University, who wrote *A Treatise on the Law of Evidence*, considered the classic work on the rules of evidence in American jurisprudence. Applying these rules to the testimony of the disciples regarding the resurrection of Jesus, he wrote a second volume entitled *An Examination of the Testimony of the Four Evangelists: The Gospels Examined by the Rules of Evidence.* Greenleaf made the following observations:

> The great truths which the apostles declared, were that Christ had risen from the dead, and that only through repentance from sin, and faith in him, could men hope for salvation. This doctrine they asserted with one voice, everywhere, not only under the greatest discouragements, but in the face of the most appalling terrors that can be presented to the mind of man. Their master had recently perished as a malefactor, by the sentence of public tribunal. His religion sought to overthrow the religions of the whole world. The laws of every country were against the teachings of his disciples. The interests and passions of all the rulers and great men in the world were against them. The fashion of the world was against them. Propagating this new faith, even in the most inoffensive and peaceful manner, they could expect nothing but contempt, opposition, revilings, bitter persecutions, stripes, imprisonments, torments, and cruel deaths. Yet this faith they zealously did propagate; and all these miseries they endured undismayed, nay, rejoicing. As one after another was put to a miserable death, the survivors only prosecuted their work with increased vigor and resolution. The annals of military warfare afford scarcely an example of the like heroic constancy, patience, and unblenching courage. They had every possible motive to review carefully the grounds of their faith, and the evidences of the great facts and truths which they asserted; and these motives were pressed upon their attention with the most melancholy and terrific frequency. It was therefore impossible that they could have persisted in affirming the truths they have narrated, had not Jesus actually risen

from the dead, and had they not known this fact as certainly as they knew any other fact. If it were morally possible for them to have been deceived in this matter, every human motive operated to lead them to discover and avow their error. To have persisted in so gross a falsehood, after it was known to them, was not only to encounter, for life, all the evils which man could inflict, from without, but to endure also the pangs of inward and conscious guilt; with no hope of future peace, no testimony of a good conscience, no expectation of honor or esteem among men, no hope of happiness in this life, or in the world to come.

Such conduct in the apostles would moreover have been utterly irreconcilable with the fact that they possessed the ordinary constitution of our common nature. Yet their lives do show them to have been men like all others of our race; swayed by the same motives, animated by the same hopes, affected by the same joys, subdued by the same sorrows, agitated by the same fears, and subject to the same passions, temptations, and infirmities, as ourselves. And their writings show them to have been men of vigorous understandings. If then their testimony was not true, there was no possible motive for its fabrication.[9]

Despite this critical assessment, there are still those who argue that a bodily resurrection is not necessary for one to believe that Jesus is alive, and that what really is important and what changed the disciples after his death was his "Spirit life" living within them. Is this really a logical alternative? The next chapter will address this issue.

---

[9] Simon Greenleaf, "The Testimony of the Evangelists," at www.bibleteacher.org/sgtestimony.htm. Greenleaf lived 1783–1853; he wrote this essay in 1847. Of additional value is the commentary by attorney Robert R. Edwards entitled, "Is Simon Greenleaf Still Relevant?" (www.creationstudies.org/Education/simon_greenleaf.html).

6

WAS A BODILY RESURRECTION REALLY NECESSARY?

The practice of medicine cannot be successfully accomplished without careful observation. Anyone who has ever been to a physician is well aware of the two-part examination that is conducted, the first being the "history," in which questions are asked to learn about the patient's complaints and what initiated them, and the second being the "physical," in which a careful bodily examination is carried out using the powers of observation to ascertain why the complaints may be occurring. No matter how thorough the history may be, no meaningful conclusions can be reached without the physical. It is the observation of the patient's body during the physical examination that puts the complaints into context and allows a "working" diagnosis to be made. Usually a series of blood tests, and sometimes x-rays, are needed to either confirm or disaffirm the proposed diagnosis, but some operational diagnosis is required before a physician knows how to proceed.

In many respects, confirming a resurrection requires similar steps. While an empty tomb and undisturbed grave clothes give hints that a resurrection may have occurred, it is the personal accounts of the witnesses who have *seen* the individual who presumably rose from the dead that give meaning to these hints and makes the diagnosis of a resurrection much more secure. Like the physical examination, which requires the senses of seeing, touching, smelling, and hearing to make a diagnosis, sensory observation is mandatory to prove a resurrection.

It has been the premise of this book that the resurrection of Jesus was a bodily one. By this I mean that when he appeared to his followers it was not in some "spiritual or visionary sense" but in an actual body. This body was fully recognizable as belonging to him and capable of interacting with other bodies in real "space-time" relationships. Thus, just as our bodies are able to interact with the bodies of our friends through the physical senses, the disciples and friends of Jesus were able to interact with him in a similar way. Not only could he be seen as a three-dimensional reality, but he could be talked to and could respond appropriately to such auditory stimulation, be touched and feel such tactile stimulation, and be perceived and identified through his physical features and body language as the same Jesus after his resurrection that he was prior to his death. He was not an apparition or ghost or figment of the imagination, but a real human being with all the features characteristic of such a being. As evidence that the resurrected Jesus possessed a real body, the New Testament Gospels indicate that this body could talk, walk, touch others, respond appropriately to emotional stimuli, and even eat.[1] In short, everything that your body and mine are capable of doing, his body could do as well.

Why is verifying the existence of such a resurrection body so important? At least three reasons can be offered. First, *it is really the only means of validating that a resurrection actually occurred.* Think for a moment what you would require of someone you knew who had died and said he would rise from the dead several days later. Hearing a strange voice out of nowhere claiming to be that person, or seeing a ghostly figure in a room that looked like that person might startle you and make you wonder whether that person really had come back to life, but by no means would these intrusions provide any concrete assurance that a resurrection had occurred. Until you actually saw a body that you could personally evaluate and examine for yourself, there would be no means to validate this alleged resurrection. Further, this body could not be just any body but would have to have the exact characteristics physically of the body you remember your friend possessing. Thus, if your deceased friend had blue eyes, this

---

[1] The ability of Jesus's post-resurrection body to talk, walk, touch others, respond emotionally, and eat is detailed in the following biblical references: Matt. 28:1–20; Mark 16:1–20; Luke 24:1–53; John 20:1–31; 21:1–25.

newly appearing body would need blue eyes. If this person had been bald, the body would need to be bald. If this person had been 6 feet 2 inches tall, the body you are now observing would have to be that height. If the deceased individual had a certain kind of tattoo on his left forearm, this body would need to have an identical tattoo. In summary, everything you can remember about your friend's body would have to be demonstrated in the body being observed.

Even if everything you are now observing seems to fit the characteristics of your deceased friend's body, this may actually be another person's body. It is here that the personality accompanying that body becomes critically important, with memory and mannerisms being especially crucial. If the person you remember laughed in a certain way, this new body should also laugh in that way. If he had told you of a secret code he used to unlock a safety deposit box, this newly appeared person should be able to reveal that code. If he went to a certain college or lived in a certain area of town, he ought to be able to state those facts without difficulty or hesitation. If he possessed certain behavior patterns when alive, such as tapping his foot or snapping his fingers during a conversation, such characteristics should be readily noticeable if this person were truly your "resurrected" friend. It should be apparent, then, from these brief examples, why a body is so necessary for validation of a resurrection, including the alleged resurrection of Jesus.

A bodily resurrection of Jesus is also important because *it is essential to adequately explain the radical transformation in thinking and attitude of the disciples from despair to a vibrant faith and the willingness to risk their lives in its proclamation.* Consider what it must have been like to be one of Jesus's disciples, and to watch him experience the brutal death to which he was subjected. One can only imagine what must have gone through their minds as his body was taken down from the cross and placed in a grave. What now? What is going to happen to us? Our leader and friend has been crucified and now is no more. All the hopes and dreams that we had when he was among us are now history. Without his leadership, everything he taught us about God's kingdom now seems irrelevant and unimportant. He made some statements about coming back to life, but what does that mean? People who die remain dead; they don't come back to life. If, by some strange happenstance, he really were able to come back to life, how would we know it had occurred? Would he look the same or be different? Would we only hear a voice, or would he actually have a body that was clearly recognizable? How would he know where to find us, if he did come back to life?

These and numerous other thoughts and questions must have run through the disciples' minds. Thus, if Jesus really did rise from the dead, there must be some means of confirming it so that his followers are assured beyond any doubt that it actually occurred. Such confirmation requires a body that can be visualized, handled, and interacted with in a real space-time dimension. It is obvious that the Gospel writers agreed with this notion, since they went to great lengths to talk about the body of Jesus in their post-resurrection accounts. As previously noted with regard to Paul's discussion of the resurrection (1 Corinthians 15), witnessing a real body was crucial to his argument that Jesus really did rise from the dead.

It cannot be emphasized too strongly that the entire mindset and attitude of the disciples was radically altered after seeing Christ's risen body. No longer were they morose and dejected. They were now joyous, self-assured, and absolutely convinced that Jesus was alive and that his message was worth proclaiming and devoting their lives to. The account of their post-resurrection activities is carefully summarized in the New Testament book of Acts. They were now bold in everything they did, willing to take chances, experience imprisonment if need be, and even be physically harmed—even to die—all in the name of their leader and Lord, Jesus Christ, whom they were absolutely convinced was alive because they had seen him in a real body. It is noteworthy that most of the sermons in the book of Acts, preached by Christ's disciples, attest to his resurrection and to having seen his post-resurrection body.

Theologian Ronald J. Sider offers these comments regarding this change in the disciples' behavior:

What gave rise to the "resurrection faith" and the disciples' willingness to risk their lives to spread it? . . . The explanation given by the people closest to the events was that Jesus of Nazareth arose from the tomb and appeared to them over a period of a number of days.

If one rejects the New Testament explanation of the resurrection faith and the transformation it caused in extremely discouraged people, then one is left with the very difficult task of proposing other grounds adequate to explain it.[2]

Sider further quotes New Testament scholar Robert M. Grant of the University of Chicago:

The origin of Christianity is almost incomprehensible unless such an event took place.[3]

It should be clear, then, that the appearance of Jesus in bodily form is the only reasonable explanation that can account for the radical change in the attitude, thinking, and commitment of the disciples following his resurrection, and their vigorous and aggressive witness on his behalf. Had such a body not manifested itself, it is safe to conclude that the hope of the disciples would have been gone forever, and this radical transformation in their personalities would not have occurred.

A third reason that a bodily resurrection is necessary is that *it not only demonstrates Jesus's post-resurrection humanity but also shows that he was much more than just human.* Being able to witness the post-resurrection body of Jesus certainly attests to his humanness, but its ability to function outside of space-time boundaries indicates that it was also uniquely different from the bodies we possess. Consider, for example, the mere fact that this body was able to rise from the dead. In all the years that I have had to deal with death, its finality has left a lasting impression with me. When a person dies, life ceases to exist. No matter what one attempts to do to communicate with a deceased person, no response is forthcoming. The reality of this deceased state

---

[2] Ronald J. Sider, "Jesus' Resurrection and the Search for Peace and Justice," *Christian Century* (November 3, 1982), 1105.
[3] Robert M. Grant, *Historical Introduction to the New Testament* (New York: Harper & Row, 1963), quoted in ibid.

is further imprinted on one's thoughts when the corpse is touched and noted to be cool and rigid (signs of rigor mortis), unable to respond to any stimulation. Equally unforgettable is the stench that exudes from dying flesh within a day or two if no effort has been made to preserve the body by freezing or embalming. The fact that Jesus was able to overcome all of these realities and present himself to witnesses in a fully verifiable body, identical in appearance and function to that which had been witnessed prior to his death, indicates that death had no hold on him. As we discussed in an earlier chapter, his ability to overcome death was not a resuscitation but a true resurrection. How was he able to do this? The only answer is that he had the capability to access "power" that could reverse what was thought to be irreversible. By doing this, he demonstrated that he was not bound by the physical laws that bind us and that the enemy death that ultimately will overcome each of us was incapable of overcoming him.

As further evidence of Jesus's ability to transcend space-time restrictions, consider his visit to his disciples when they were gathered together in a locked room. He made such a visit on two separate occasions in a fully verifiable body (see John 20:19–29). In fact, as we have seen, in the second visit he challenged the disciple Thomas to personally touch and examine the marks in his hands of the nails that had impaled him to the cross, as well as the wound in his side where the spear had pierced him. Thomas, needing to analyze everything, was so convinced with what he saw that he apparently forgot about any need to actually touch Jesus's hands and side, and instead fell down on his knees acknowledging with gratitude that the body he was viewing was that of his master, Jesus (compare John 20:25, 27–28, and see chapter 5 of this book for more discussion on Thomas). What makes these two visits even more amazing is that Jesus's body did not require an unlocked door to enter the room. Jesus simply appeared of his own accord as though he had walked through the wall. Similarly, when he exited the room on both occasions, he did not need to open a door or find a window out of which to escape. He simply disappeared as though he had evaporated. How are these things possible? They can be explained only by asserting that, while Jesus's body was fully human in one sense, it had power in another sense to do those things that only a superhuman being is capable of doing (see chapter 7 for further discussion of these superhuman qualities).

One final vignette is worth discussing. This involves the account in the first chapter of Acts where Jesus is meeting for the last time with his disciples (see Acts 1:1–11). In a purely recognizable post-resurrection body, he instructs his disciples regarding the mission on which they are about to embark—to spread the good news about him—and he then informs them that it is now time to conclude his earthly ministry and return to God the Father. Without any fanfare or preparation, he then ascended upward into the heavens and was seen no more. In short, he defied all gravitational forces and took off with a speed that required no special gear (like a space suit), thrust (like burning fuel), or vehicle (like a space shuttle), and effortlessly disappeared. How could he do this if he were *just* a man? This incident, as well as his visits to the locked room and his defiance of death, all indicate that he was more than a man. Actually, he is the God-man, just as he claimed many times when teaching his followers.[4] But this message could never be appropriately conveyed and articulated without a post-resurrection body. It is this body that validated once and for all that he was both man and God (see chapter 7). Thus, while being truly physical and material as our bodies are physical and material, Christ's body possessed characteristics that transcended the physical and material as we know it, allowing the natural and supernatural realms of reality to merge and freely interact. In short, this body exhibited a *"transformed physicality*," as N. T. Wright puts it, "with new properties and attributes but still concrete and physical."[5]

Despite these arguments for a bodily resurrection, there are still many who vehemently contest that Jesus rose from the dead in any literal sense. In their minds, the resurrection was purely "spiritual" and

---

[4] Biblical references regarding Christ's claim to be God include Matt. 26:64; Mark 2:5–12; 14:61–64; Luke 24:27; John 5:18–23; 8:58; 10:31–33; 17:5; 18:5–6, 8.

[5] To my knowledge, Wright is the first person to use this terminology to describe Jesus's post-resurrection body. See N. T. Wright, "The Transforming Reality of the Bodily Resurrection," in *The Meaning of Jesus: Two Visions*, ed. M. J. Borg and N. T. Wright (San Francisco: Harper San Francisco, 1999), 111–127.

nothing more. Such people usually take this position because they are intolerant of the miraculous and have no place for the supernatural Jesus in their worldview. Jesus to them was a great teacher and role model, but any consideration that he was "God in the flesh" is preposterous, and any possibility that he really came back to life in an actual physical/material body is absurd.

Jesus knew that there would be people who would react to his resurrection in this way. Perhaps you are one of them. To make it abundantly clear, though, that he really did possess a resurrection body that was truly physical and not spiritual, Luke records an interesting vignette that specifically addresses the physical nature of Jesus's body. During one of Jesus's encounters with his disciples following his resurrection, we are told:

> . . . Jesus himself stood among them, and said to them, "Peace to you!" But they were startled and frightened and thought they saw a spirit. And he said to them, "Why are you troubled, and why do doubts arise in your hearts? See my hands and my feet, that it is I myself. Touch me, and see. For a spirit does not have flesh and bones as you see that I have." And when he had said this, he showed them his hands and his feet. (Luke 24:36–40)

In case there remained any further doubt about his physicality, he then asked for food, to prove that he really did reside in a body, whereupon they gave him some broiled fish and he ate it in their presence (Luke 24:41–43). Three other scriptural passages also record instances of the resurrected Jesus eating with his disciples (see Luke 24:30; John 21:12–13; and the marginal reading at Acts 1:4, ESV). There should be no question, then, about the physicality of Jesus's resurrection body. One may choose to deny it, but it is clear that Jesus demonstrated its certainty to his followers.

Irrespective of these considerations, the mere concept of a "spiritual resurrection" has unique problems. It defies any precise definition or means of validation, and to believe that Jesus's disciples would base their lives on such a notion is difficult to fathom. To show the elusiveness of this view, it is instructive to consider the thinking of Bishop John Shelby

Spong, whom we met in chapter 4, who has no place for the miraculous in his theological worldview, clearly dismissing the idea of Jesus rising from the dead in a physical body. In commenting on the Gospel accounts of Jesus's resurrection, Spong says that they are legendary stories developed over time by "literal-minded" people because of the need to speak of God and things of the spirit through human words. He does not dispute that something dramatic happened to the disciples of Jesus following his death that radically changed them; otherwise the birth of Christianity would not have occurred. Whatever this "something" was, however, in Spong's mind it clearly was not the appearance of Jesus in a resurrected body. Rather, he contends that "Jesus was raised from death into God" and out of this transformation Jesus appeared to his disciples in a kind of "heavenly vision." It was this "spirit presence of Jesus" that made them alive in a new way, convincing them that the Jesus they had known prior to his death was now very much alive again. Through the power of that experience, they could shout without equivocation that "Jesus Lives!"[6]

From Spong's perspective it was not a physical resurrection that prompted the assurance in the disciples that "Jesus lives," but rather a conviction of the spiritual presence of the living Jesus, which Spong calls the "Spirit Person" Jesus. With all due respect to Spong, I personally would not find such an understanding of the resurrection at all reassuring or comforting if I had been one of the disciples, especially if I knew that the Jesus I had been following for the previous three years was a dead corpse in some grave, as Spong apparently believes. Further, if this so-called spiritual presence really was the meaning of resurrection, how would I know for certain it was Jesus's presence and not a figment of my own imagination—because I really wanted Jesus to be alive? This sounds too much like a "Casper the Friendly Ghost" phenomenon. If this is what the resurrection is supposed to mean, I stand unconvinced.

---

[6] John Shelby Spong, *Why Christianity Must Change or Die* (New York: Harper Collins, 1999), 116–117; Other contemporary writers who believe in a "spiritual resurrection" include Marcus Borg and John Dominic Crossan, who argue along the same lines as Spong; see M. J. Borg, "The Truth of Easter," in Borg and Wright, eds., *Meaning of Jesus*, 129–142; J. D. Crossan, *Jesus: A Revolutionary Biography* (San Francisco: HarperSanFrancisco, 1994).

Besides this vagueness and lack of objective validation, the other issue that needs to be dealt with by those who believe in a spiritual resurrection and insist that Jesus's body is dead relates to the mystery of the empty tomb. To claim that the empty tomb was a concocted story that evolved many years after Jesus's death simply does not fit the overwhelming consensus of contemporary New Testament scholarship. Many respected scholars have argued compellingly that the Gospels were written much earlier (see chapter 2) than Spong and others who share his viewpoint are willing to admit, thus lessening the possibility of their being based on mere legend. All four Gospels are consistent in saying that the tomb was empty. While an empty tomb by itself does not prove a physical resurrection, as we discussed in chapter 4, it cannot be ignored and needs to have a rational explanation. On the other hand, if Jesus really is dead and his corpse resides in a Palestinian grave, the evidence for this contention requires appropriate documentation. For some two thousand years now, no such evidence has been forthcoming. Thus, as a person seeking verifiable evidence, I am unconvinced by the metaphorical interpretation that Jesus is somehow among us spiritually even though physically he is dead.

Further, the teaching of the disciples concerning the resurrection, as recorded in the book of Acts, the earliest history of the Christian church, makes no sense if Jesus did not rise from the dead in a physical body. The inaugural sermon preached by the apostle Peter is quite certain on this issue (see Acts 2:14–39). In comparing the death and burial of King David with that of Jesus, Peter makes it abundantly clear that David was still dead and buried whereas Jesus's body was not abandoned to the grave to see decay but was raised to life by God, of which "we all are witnesses" (v. 32). To conclude that this is all legend, as Spong and others would like us to believe, goes against the consensus of contemporary biblical scholarship (both conservative and liberal), which attests that Acts had to be written before the death of the apostle Paul (mid-60s AD) and the destruction of Jerusalem by the Romans (AD 70), since neither of these events are discussed in Acts as one would logically expect if it had been written after those events had occurred (see chapter 2). In their book *Resurrection—Truth and*

Reality: Three Scholars Reply to Bishop Spong," Paul Barnett, Peter Jensen, and David Peterson offer these compelling insights:

> The notion that Jesus was resurrected in a totally spiritual sense, while his old body lay in the grave, is a *purely modern conception.* First-century Jewish thinking would never had [*sic*] accepted such a view and that is not how Jesus' resurrection was proclaimed in the earliest accounts. It would have been impossible for resurrection claims to survive in the face of a tomb containing the corpse of Jesus.[7]

N. T. Wright reaches similar conclusions in his historical analysis of first-century Jewish culture. He notes,

> Resurrection implies at the very least a coming *back* to something that had been forfeited, that is, bodily life. . . . What the early church insisted about Jesus was that he had been well and truly physically dead and was now well and truly physically alive.[8]

Thus, any presumption that Jesus was raised from the dead in some "spiritual" sense, rather than physically, is a total misrepresentation of the Jewish understanding of a resurrection during the time when Jesus walked among us.

Finally, it must be remembered that the disciples were "hard-nosed" practical men. Most of them were fishermen who worked long hours for a living and in today's terminology would be called "blue collar" workers. For them life was "black and white" and "either/or." Basically, they were "bottom-line" people who wanted everything told like it is. Metaphors and similes belonged to the world of the philosophers and academics. Their world was one of sight, hearing, and touching. They functioned in real time and three dimensions. They wanted to hear it with their own ears, see it with their own eyes, and touch it with their own hands. To live in the world of abstract ideas and appearances was foreign to them. They wanted everything spelled out so they knew whether to move forward or move on to something

---

[7] Paul Barnett, Peter Jensen, and David Peterson, *Resurrection—Truth and Reality: Three Scholars Reply to Bishop Spong* (Sydney: Aquila, 1994), 14.
[8] Wright, "Transforming Reality of the Bodily Resurrection," 116.

else. It is for these reasons that they needed and expected a bodily resurrection rather than some ethereal concept, idea, symbol, or figurative language to prove that their leader was alive. If Jesus really did rise from the dead, they needed to see him, talk to him, and touch him. Anything less would be unconvincing.

We started this chapter with the question "Was a bodily resurrection really necessary?" We end with a resounding answer of yes! The evidence clearly shows that a body, identical in all respects to that which existed prior to death, is absolutely crucial if a resurrection is to be validated. The Gospels have provided that evidence in a compelling and convincing way, indicating that Jesus really did rise from the dead.

7

WHAT DOES A RESURRECTION MEAN?

"Okay," you say, "I agree that the evidence is convincing, perhaps even compelling, that Jesus did in fact rise from the dead in a literal body. So what? Of what significance is this event to me personally?" Before answering these questions directly, it is important to make some additional comments concerning death, and especially those barriers that would need to be overcome for a dead person actually to come back to life.

To fully grasp the meaning of a resurrection, it is absolutely crucial to mentally and emotionally come to grips with the finality and irreversibility of death. It is one thing to learn of a friend's "passing" and to respond in a casual way, sending a note of sympathy and a suitable floral arrangement. It is quite another to attend the funeral and go with the remaining "loved ones" to the burial. As one reflects, during all those proceedings, on what has actually happened, the reality of the situation is silently imprinted on one's consciousness. The person who was once a living, breathing human being is now gone and is not coming back. No matter how much one might have wished otherwise, it would be ludicrous to expect the individual in the casket to leap back to life. The finality of death becomes even more sobering upon going to the cemetery and witnessing the lowering of the casket into the previously dug gravesite, and then watching the soil cover the casket. If there had ever been any doubt as to whether the person in the casket was indeed dead, all doubts cease at that point.

What if a person whose death you had witnessed, and whose

funeral and burial you had attended, were to personally appear before you one week later? I am not talking about a dream or apparition, but a real appearance of this individual in a physical body, so that you could see him in the same way you did prior to his death. You could talk to him, shake his hand, observe him walking, eat with him, and he would respond appropriately. What would you think? After getting over the shock of it all, you would have to conclude either that he had not died or that through some unknown process he had come back to life. Since you know the former option is not a possibility, having attended his funeral and burial, the only logical conclusion is that your friend is once again alive. While I realize that you have never been confronted with such an event, try to imagine how you would react if someone you knew actually did come back to life. Your thoughts about this "come back to life" person would most certainly be very different than how you envisioned him prior to his death. Imagining such a scenario, several things immediately come to mind.

Power, Knowledge, and Authority

First, however his resurrection actually occurred, the fact that it did occur tells me that this person is able to "tap into" or is linked in some way with a realm of power quite unlike anything I know naturally. In short, he has access to a power that defies any human explanation. From a physiological perspective, several barriers immediately need to be overcome for a dead person to come back to life. The initial barrier is the need to return dead cells to life. In the many years I conducted laboratory research, the focus of my studies was on those processes by which gastrointestinal cells (those from the lining of the stomach or intestine) protected themselves against injury. In working with such cells, I was continually amazed with how fragile they were. To keep them alive and healthy in order to enable me to study them, they had to be carefully grown in a culture medium so that they received the essential nutrients necessary for life. In addition, the right amount of oxygen had to be administered to ensure that life processes within the cells were maintained and the energy needed for these processes was provided. If anything detrimental happened to these cells, such as exposure to a toxic substance, they usually died quickly (often within minutes) and nothing I did could change this circumstance. If perchance I were able to alter the adverse effects of the toxin, I might be able to prevent the cells from dying and thus proceed with my experiment, but once they were dead, any attempt to reenergize them was futile.

On a much larger and more complex scale, think of a human body that has died. This body contains literally trillions of cells (some scientists believe as many as 100 trillion) with each of these cells being able to carry out thousands of different chemical reactions and their associated functions.[1] To bring a body back to life once it has died, some phenomenal power would not only have to energize "life" into all these individual cells, but it would have to do so in such a way that specialized nerve cells could resume their unique function, heart cells perform theirs, blood cells and bone cells do theirs, and so on. Obviously, such a life-giving power is outside the realm of anything we humans possess or even know about. We would have to conclude not only that the power that could cause such a resurrection is superhuman, but that the hypothetical person we are discussing is somehow able to tap into this power and experience its life-energizing capabilities.

But that's not all. Once life has been infused into this corpse, this resurrected body has to be released from the casket in which it is housed, six feet or so below the earth's surface. The walls of the casket, the hundreds of pounds of soil on top of it, and the gravitational pull of the earth must be overcome to allow this resurrected corpse to escape. The fact that this resurrection power can circumvent these barriers indicates that it is much more all-encompassing than might have been appreciated. It not only has life-giving capabilities but is also able to overcome many other forces of nature.

It is one thing to play this imagination game, since none of us

---

[1] B. Alberts, A. Johnson, J. Lewis, M. Raff, K. Roberts, and P. Walter, *Molecular Biology of the Cell*, 4th ed. (New York: Garland Science, 2002) (1463 pages); J. E. Hall. *Guyton and Hall Textbook of Medical Physiology*, 12th ed. (Philadelphia: SaundersElsevier, 2011) (1120 pages). These two textbooks are commonly used in most medical schools in the United States to explain the sophistication of cellular function involving the trillions of cells in our bodies, and how this cellular function impacts organ function.

have ever seen a resurrection nor are we anticipating that one of our deceased friends will return to life. It is quite another thing, however, to realize that this is exactly what Jesus did, namely, overcome the forces of death and any attendant barriers (such as the encircling grave clothes and the barricaded tomb) to demonstrate that death had been conquered. To even attempt to understand the power necessary to make that happen, or to try to visualize how it happened, is incomprehensible and mind-boggling. Nothing I have ever experienced comes even close to any concept of the power needed to bring a dead person back to life. Thus, in seeking to characterize the meaning of the resurrection, *limitless power* (perhaps even best described as "cosmic power") is clearly a designation that has to be included. But where did this power come from, and what or who is responsible for harnessing it?

Before attempting to answer these questions, two other considerations must be addressed. First is the issue of *knowledge*. It is one thing to have limitless power to effect a resurrection, but it is quite another to take a body with all its incredible complexity and sophistication and, once it is dead, to put it back together so that it can function again. Of the trillions of cells that comprise a body's makeup, thousands of biochemical reactions within each cell are operational every moment to make sure that each organ system functions optimally and does so in coordination with all the other organs, so that everything proceeds in synchrony. Consider the heart as just one example. It beats on average 70 times a minute, 4,200 times an hour, 100,800 times a day, 3,024,000 times a month, and 36,288,000 times a year. If a person lives to eighty, the heart has beaten some 3 billion times. And for that to happen, thousands of processes within each cell must act in a coordinated way to ensure that the blood entering the right side of the heart is effectively propelled to the lungs, where the red blood cells contained in it discharge carbon dioxide and pick up oxygen, following which it returns to the left side of the heart where it is subsequently propelled to the tissues of the rest of the body, so that they might receive the precious oxygen they need to sustain their many functions. This all happens at least every second in such a smooth fashion that we are not even aware of it. And yet the moment we die, all these processes come to a screeching halt.

It should not be surprising, then, that extraordinary knowledge is needed to rebuild a dead body and bring it back to life, Jesus's body being no exception. The incredible number of processes necessary to make that body function again had to be restarted, and this had to be done in such a way that the synchrony that existed prior to death would be reinstated. This presumes that the source of knowledge making that happen is fully familiar with the details of each one of these processes and knows how to make them happen. But remember, we are not talking about several dozen processes or even a hundred or so; we are talking about thousands of processes within each cell, all with their unique intricacy and need for careful inter-coordination.

Even the latest science has not unraveled the complete mystery of each of the cells of our bodies, and how they interact with and "talk" to one another. While we know much about cellular function, there is still much more to learn—and most certainly untapped mysteries that we presently know nothing about. But for the resurrection of Jesus to occur, all of that information had to be known in its completeness and totality, and known some two thousand years ago. When we consider all that has been learned about the physiology of the human body in general and its cellular makeup in particular over just the past two or three decades, how could any of this information have been known in the first century? It obviously had to be known, however, to bring the dead body of Jesus back to life.

The final issue requiring explanation is that of *authority*. Or to put it another way, whence comes the authority to use this power and knowledge to effect a resurrection? No matter how senior one may be in his place of employment, unless he himself is the "boss," he is accountable to someone. Limitless freedom without accountability leads to chaos. Even a boss, if he does not exercise his authority properly, can destroy his company. Long-lasting and productive institutions virtually always have strong leaders.

How does all of this relate to the issue of resurrection? We have seen that Jesus's resurrection could occur only by a power capable of bringing a dead body back to life. We have also seen that there would have to be a complete understanding of the sophistication and complexity of all the processes that make the human body work, how these processes interact, and basically how to "jump-start" them again once the dead cells of the body are brought back to life. Additionally, a complete understanding of all these processes would have had to be known in the first century when the resurrection occurred, despite the fact that our understanding even now, twenty centuries later, is at best incomplete. Finally, this power and knowledge would have had to be present, effected instantaneously, and coordinated perfectly and flaw-lessly so as not to disrupt the laws of nature in any significant way. In short, something or someone with sovereign authority would need to activate all of this.

So how can this all occur and be orchestrated without error if a resurrection is to happen? We all know that power can be either exceedingly beneficial or incredibly destructive, depending on how it is used. When untamed, it can become a devastating and life-threat-ening tornado, hurricane, or tsunami. When channeled productively, though, something as basic as water can be used to generate electrical power, as occurs in a hydroelectric plant, which then can be applied to meeting all kinds of needs. Similarly, fossil fuels can be retrieved and purified to manufacture gasoline to power our cars and gas to heat our homes. Our modern era has mastered the power of informa-tion technology by building computers and programming them for retrieval and dissemination of incredible amounts of information, with no end to possible applications. Although many other examples of the productive harnessing of power could be cited, common to all of them is the creative thought and genius of the human *mind* to make them happen; they don't just spontaneously occur. Similarly, knowl-edge by itself is nothing more than a collection of words in a book or on a computer screen, or information that may have been obtained through a lecture or seminar that has no relevance until it is assimi-lated, interpreted, and applied to some use, again requiring the activ-ity of a *mind*. Finally, there is the issue of authority: One may have the requisite knowledge and power to carry out something, but until the appropriate authorization has been obtained to allow "follow-through," it will not happen. Like power and knowledge, authority is not some inanimate, ill-defined force or energy, but assumes a *mind* to carry out whatever was requiring authorization.

Now return to the issue of the resurrection of Jesus. For it to occur, there had to be a *mind* behind it. This mind not only had to understand the power necessary to make it possible; it also had to have the requisite knowledge to make sure that all the relevant processes would be up and running in each of the cells of this resurrection body. Finally, since dead people do not come back to life in our "natural world," the authority characterized by this mind would have to be able to freely overcome whatever natural laws or barriers would stand in the way of bringing Jesus's dead body back to life. And this would have to have been accomplished without disrupting the smooth running of Planet Earth, so that human life and activity in other respects would proceed normally.

How is such a stupendous event to be explained? It obviously did not occur through some blind, indifferent, spontaneous process. As already noted, all the issues regarding power, knowledge, and authority to make a resurrection happen imply the existence of a mind. And this mind, at the very least, had to have as part of its makeup some very unique characteristics. Among these would be *omnipotence* (the state of having unlimited, unrestricted power); *omniscience* (the state of having infinite understanding, awareness, and complete and universal knowledge); and *sovereignty* (complete autonomy and freedom from external control). The only mind that can be adequately defined as having such qualities is the mind of a *sovereign God*, and not just any god but *the God* who is responsible for flinging this universe into existence with his creative powers and who has total control over every aspect of it.

Someone might object at this point that all the emphasis on the cellular makeup of Jesus's post-resurrection body is a bit much. After all, the argument might go, "Isn't the *appearance* of the body the important issue? If the resurrection body looked like Jesus and was really indistinguishable from how Jesus appeared in his pre-deceased state, isn't that enough to prove that a resurrection occurred?" Yes and no. Yes, in the sense that the body we are talking about would certainly have to look like Jesus if we are to convince anyone that it was his body, but many could say that this look-alike body was nothing more than an apparition or hallucination. While bodily appearance is important, equally important is the demonstration of bodily function, and that function exhibiting itself in space and time and three-dimensionally. In that sense, the answer to the above question is no. The mere appearance of a resurrected body is not sufficient evidence. Take, for example, the ability of a body to eat, as Jesus did on a number of occasions with his disciples after the resurrection. To eat involves a digestive tract. And if this body is human, a digestive tract includes an esophagus, stomach, small intestine, large intestine, and organs like the liver, gall bladder, and pancreas that assist in the digestion and assimilation of foods. All of these organs, in turn, are made up of billions of cells with differing functions depending on which organ they are a part of.

Jesus also talked and walked. Talking requires a larynx (voice box), and neck and facial muscles to move air so that speech is produced. Walking requires bones and muscles so that purposeful movement results. In each of these circumstances, the structures involved are made up of cells with diverse responsibilities to ensure that the activity for which they were intended is carried out successfully.

And don't forget that who we are as a body is determined by our DNA (deoxyribonucleic acid). This molecule contains the genetic code of each human, the biological instructions that make you and me what we are and determine how we look. DNA is what makes you precisely you, and me precisely me. And interestingly, the DNA responsible for this uniqueness is housed in the command center of each of our cells, known as the nucleus. Thus, if there are no cells, there are no DNA command centers. This is why *appearance and function* are interlinked and are both necessary to prove that a bodily resurrection actually happened. While the appearance of a body lends credence to the contention that a resurrection may have occurred, these functional considerations play a key role in validating it.

I fully accept that a sovereign God can create a resurrection body in any way he desires. From the standpoint of recognition, though, it would have to be identical to how Jesus "looked" and "functioned" in the pre-deceased state to ensure that it really was he. The fact that more than 500 witnesses testified that the resurrected Jesus was the same Jesus they had known prior to his death indicates that there was true "continuity," as theologians call it, between his pre- and post-resurrection body in terms of appearance. It is my contention, based on my understanding of the human body and how it works, that this continuity was evident not only with respect to outward appearance but also with respect to bodily function, and as such characterized every tissue and organ of his body (and the cells responsible for them). Jesus said his body would be destroyed and then would be raised again in three days (see John 2:19–22). Implicit in this assertion is that the body raised is the same one that was destroyed. Further, the testimony of the early church affirmed that his resurrection body was the same one he possessed before his death (see Acts 2:29–36).

These things being said, there also was "discontinuity" between Jesus's pre- and post-resurrection bodies, meaning that his resurrection body had capabilities and features that his body prior to death did not possess (see Paul's discussion of the resurrection body in 1 Cor. 15:35–49). The stunning characteristic of this difference was first and foremost the ability of his resurrection body to overcome death, because it was now "*animated by* a new type of life," as Wright puts it.[2] The "ordinary life-force" that energized Christ's pre-resurrection body had now been replaced with a new energy that was clearly supernatural. Whereas it had been corruptible (subject to aging and decay) and mortal (subject to death) before, it was now incorruptible and immortal. Whereas it had been weak and limited in power before, it now exhibited limitless power and the strength never to die again. While this resurrection body could easily function in space and time as it had in its pre-resurrection state, it was not restricted by these bar-

---

[2] N. T. Wright, "The Transformed Resurrection Body," in *Paul for Everyone: I Corinthians* (Louisville: Westminster John Knox, 2004), 219–224. This is an excellent discussion of the transformed resurrection body. My own comments are a brief distillation of some of Wright's discussion.

riers anymore and demonstrated unique features such as being able to appear and disappear at will, and to walk through closed doors. His effortless ascension to heaven upon completion of his earthly ministry is yet another example of this discontinuity. What are we to make of these findings? While Jesus's resurrection body was very much a physical body in one sense, it was clearly "transformed" with supernatural qualities in another sense. As we noted in the previous chapter, the only way to adequately describe Jesus's resurrection body is to call it a *transformed physicality*. Again, for such a transformed body to be fashioned, the *mind* of a sovereign God was necessary. Truly, such a body could only exist if energized by God's Spirit!

Implications of the Resurrection

If a sovereign God was responsible for Jesus's resurrection, a number of assertions can be made. *First*, any doubt about the existence of God as a real being is forever nullified; accepting the resurrection as a real event likewise means that *God is real*. One may reject the evidence for the resurrection, but even then the skeptic can only say that God "might not" exist; lack of a resurrection does not prove God's *nonexistence*. Although many of my scientific colleagues who have declared themselves atheists or agnostics would like to put the God issue behind them, the blunt fact is that science does not permit us to draw any conclusions about God's existence one way or another. It can neither prove nor disprove his existence. The resurrection, on the other hand, stands out as an event that screams loudly for God's existence.

The *second* assertion contends that there is such a thing as the *supernatural*. While this word can be defined in various ways, in the context of the present discussion it refers to "an order of existence beyond the visible, observable universe." When we think of the world in which we live, observation is absolutely crucial to understanding it; indeed, observation is the backbone of modern scientific inquiry. Employing the powers of observation, we form hypotheses as to how our world functions, we test these hypotheses to determine whether they will hold up to rigorous analysis, and then we draw conclusions as to what our findings mean and whether they validate our original interpretation of what we observed. Using such an approach, knowledge concerning our universe and the laws that govern it has mushroomed over the past several centuries. In the last fifty years alone, this knowledge has grown exponentially. It is little wonder, then, that science reigns supreme and has become a major (some would say *the* major) means of seeking truth.

So is the supernatural really believable? Many scientists would answer no; many others would say probably not, but if there is a supernatural realm, there is no way of confirming it using scientific methods. Precisely at this juncture, the resurrection takes on important meaning. The resurrection of Jesus clearly demonstrates that there really is a supernatural realm. While we may not understand it and have no means of studying it as we do the natural world, the resurrection puts to rest any misgivings regarding the existence of the supernatural. This single event validates once and for all the certainty of a supernatural order of reality.

A *third* assertion emanating from the resurrection is that the *miraculous* is no longer just a figment of the imagination. If God can raise a dead body to life again, he has already demonstrated that he can supersede the laws of nature to accomplish his purposes without interrupting the stability of the cosmos in the process. How is this possible? It assumes that he is the creative genius behind the cosmos; that he made it all possible, including life itself; that he has established the laws that govern it; and that he can temporarily interrupt or modify those laws to accomplish what we commonly call miracles. Obviously these interventions are uncommon, or the laws of nature would have no meaning and the cosmos would have no stability. How often miracles take place is known only to God, for they occur in accordance with his will as the sovereign of the universe. Nevertheless, if there was any doubt about the possibility of miracles, the resurrection has proved that doubt to be unfounded.

Finally, a *fourth* assertion linked with Jesus's resurrection is the concept of the *eternal*. We humans are temporal beings and define everything we do in terms of time. We celebrate our birthdays annually and look at life and its various stages as a collection of years. Depending on our age we call ourselves children, adolescents, young adults, middle-aged, elderly, or we say that we are in our "twilight" years. As much as we would wish otherwise, we know full well that time marches on and eventually we will die. Our response to this prospect is greatly influenced by our worldview. We may look at death as the end of our existence or as the entrance into some type of afterlife. Again, the resurrection clarifies any ambiguity or uncertainty regarding this issue.

Even though Jesus functioned in our space-time world during the thirty-three years that he lived among us, the resurrection clearly demonstrated that he cannot be defined in strictly temporal terms. This is in contrast to every other human being, including you and me, whose lives can best be described as an interval between two points in time—birth and death. The fact that Jesus overcame death indicates that he is not bound by this universal event that will ultimately claim the rest of us. The only word that adequately captures this state of endless existence is *eternal* or its synonym *everlasting*. Little wonder then that the great British author and poet G. K. Chesterton referred to Jesus as the "Everlasting Man."[3]

This eternality of Jesus also challenges the common contemporary notion that human life ceases after one's death. As noted throughout this book, many in the scientific community firmly believe that death is the end of life for humans, just as it is for animals—once dead, always dead. But is that necessarily true, since there is no way to prove such an assertion scientifically? If a sovereign God could raise Jesus from the dead, why is he restricted from raising others from the dead, you and me included? The resurrection declared that death had been defeated, and that life after death was no longer a theoretical concept but a reality. The idea that death is the end of man's existence has now been overthrown; the life after death demonstrated in Jesus's resurrection is no longer just a hope but a certainty. In fact the Christian religion, in its creeds and confessions, adamantly states that there is

---

[3]G. K. Chesterton, *The Everlasting Man* (1925; repr., San Francisco: Ignatius, 1993).

life after death, and that how we live in this life and the decisions we make while alive impact what happens to us in the next. Nonexistence after death is not an option, if the Christian worldview is correct. Thus, Jesus's resurrection has important eternal implications for us personally.

Who Is This Jesus?

The early Christians firmly believed that God raised Jesus from the dead (see Acts 2:24–32; 10:40; 13:30; Rom. 8:9–11; 10:9; 2 Cor. 4:14). If this is true, as we have argued, who is this Jesus, that he alone, of all mankind, should experience resurrection? One need only peruse the New Testament Gospel accounts detailing his life, and clues providing the answer to this question quickly emerge. Jesus was born under miraculous circumstances to a virgin named Mary, and was worshiped at the time of his birth as being "sent from God." Although usually referred to as Jesus (meaning "God saves"), he was also called Immanuel (meaning "God with us"). In John's Gospel, he is referred to as the Word who was with God and who was God, and through whom all things were made (see John 1:1–4). John further states that, even though no one has seen God, this Word became flesh and lived among us, and as God's only Son he made God known to us (John 1:14, 18). At the time of Jesus's baptism, a voice from heaven declared him to be God's Son with whom he is well pleased (Matt. 3:16–17). Although much can be said about Jesus's earthly life from the Gospel accounts, several things are especially noteworthy. Jesus seemed to have a sense of purpose and authority in everything he did, and when people were around him they felt fearless and secure. His character was impeccable, and virtue was exhibited in everything he did. Although people were not always pleased with what he said, they could find no fault or hypocrisy in him. He demonstrated unusual power both in what he taught and in his interactions with people. In fact, many of these actions can only be described as miraculous, including the feeding of five thousand people with five loaves and two fishes, changing water into wine, calming a treacherous storm on the Sea of Galilee, casting out demons, and healing a multitude of diseases ranging from blindness to paralysis to actually raising people from the dead. His power to accomplish such things seemed effortless. Interestingly, he also claimed to forgive sins—something, supposedly, that only God can do.

Of special note, concerning Jesus, is the frequency with which he linked himself to God. He often said things like, "Whoever has seen me has seen the Father [referring to God]," "I and the Father are one," and, "No one comes to the Father except through me" (John 14:9; 10:30; 14:6). He even quoted Old Testament Scriptures and stated that specific passages referred to him and were fulfilled in him. On several occasions, he predicted his own death, but also firmly stated that he would rise from the dead; he spoke with absolute certainty that these things would happen. Finally, just before he bowed his head and died on the cross, a Roman soldier standing nearby made this stunning assertion: "Truly this was the Son of God!" (Matt. 27:54).

What are we to make of all of this? Is Jesus a madman, deluded, or an egomaniac? If the resurrection had not occurred, it would be easy to say that Jesus was no different than you or me with the possible exception of having delusions of grandeur about himself. The resurrection, however, excludes those possibilities. It makes no sense that a sovereign God would raise Jesus from the dead if he wasn't pleased with who he was and how he had lived his life. The only logical conclusion about this Jesus is that he really was "God in the flesh" as the Gospels claim. The apostle Paul asserts that because Jesus humbled himself and became obedient, even to the point of dying a brutal death on the cross, God has highly exalted him and given him a "name that is above every name, so that at the name of Jesus every knee should bow, . . . and every tongue confess that Jesus Christ is Lord, to the glory of God the Father" (Phil. 2:8–11).

If Jesus truly was God, as the New Testament asserts and the Christian church from its beginning has proclaimed, at least three affirmations logically follow. *First*, not only does God exist, as stated previously, but he has allowed himself to be known. By living among us in our space-time world, Jesus declared by his very life that God is not some impersonal force or abstract power that resides somewhere "out there" after having brought the universe into existence, never to be known in any tangible way except as some indescribable energy or force. Rather, he is fully knowable, and he has chosen to reveal himself in the person of Jesus. This is why the resurrection is such a pivotal event in human history. Had the resurrection not occurred, Jesus would have been no different from any other religious leader, and his claims about being God in the flesh would have been rightly interpreted as hollow proclamations of a self-deceived charlatan. But the resurrection changed all of that. Jesus's rising from the dead actually sets him apart not only from every other religious leader who has ever lived, but from every human being who has ever lived. The resurrection validates for all time that he is indeed God in the flesh. Thus, as he indicated on multiple occasions, "Whoever has seen me has seen the Father," since "I and the Father are one" (John 10:30; 14:9).[4]

The *second* affirmation is that the God-man Jesus demonstrates the personhood of God. When Jesus, the very essence of God, entered our world, he did not come as some strange creature from outer space who knew nothing about the human condition, but rather he came as a full-fledged human, experiencing everything that you and I have experienced. The whole story of his life, from birth to death as recorded in the Gospels, is a continuous panorama of experiences like ours. Thus, if we want to know how God thinks and acts in the human arena, we need only look at Jesus and examine his life when he walked among us. This "incarnation," as theologians refer to Christ's taking on human flesh, demonstrates a God who fully understands us and can empathize with our pain and sorrow as well as our joy and happiness.

Third, this God made known in Jesus calls us into relationship with himself. It is impossible to read the Gospel accounts of Jesus's earthly ministry without appreciating the importance he placed on human relationships. People were not objects, or things, or case studies, but persons of utmost value and significance because they were created in God's image to have purposeful and meaningful lives.

---

[4] Other Biblical passages emphasizing that Jesus is God include Mark 2:7–10; John 20:25–29; John 13:3; John 8:57–58; John 13:19.

Thus, when the God-man Jesus encountered human need, irrespective of how it expressed itself, he did not write it off as inconsequential in the "total scheme of things." Rather, he met this need "head on" and identified at a very personal level with the individual experiencing the need. Sometimes the need required healing. At other times it required a word of encouragement or reassurance. At still other times it was best met by simply listening and allowing the individual to express some deep-seated guilt or internal struggle. Regardless of the complexity of the problem, Jesus was never in a hurry or too busy to deal with the problem, and he always demonstrated boundless love and compassion to the one going through the struggle.

So what does a resurrection mean? At the very least it affirms the existence of a sovereign God. It also indicates that there is a supernatural realm of reality, that miracles are possible, and that the eternal is not a theoretical concept but a certainty. It further affirms that the recipient of this resurrection, namely Jesus, truly was the Son of God and thus the manifestation of God in the flesh. If his incarnation twenty centuries ago was intended to make God known, reveal his personhood, and demonstrate his desire for human relationship, what does all of this have to do with you and me, living in the twenty-first century? Actually everything, for it shouts forth God's desire to have us know him, so that he can enable us to be everything for which we were created! Where does Jesus's crucifixion fit into this picture? Was there also a purpose behind his death, or was it simply an unfortunate execution at the hands of those who hated him and his ministry and wanted him destroyed? Could it be that this death was part of God's grand scheme to make a personal relationship between us humans and himself possible? The answer to all these questions has tremendous relevance concerning the meaning of life itself and forms the basis of the discussion in our next chapter.

8

JESUS'S DEATH: AN ACCIDENT OF HISTORY, OR DIVINELY PLANNED?

Christianity is built on two historical events that occurred in our space-time world: the cruel death of Jesus by crucifixion on our behalf, and his ability to overcome that death by bodily resurrection. For nearly two thousand years the proclamation of these two events has been the backbone of the Christian message. Billions of people have embraced this message over the centuries, and many have given their lives in its defense. At the present time, at least 2 billion people worldwide call themselves Christians. The original disciples of Jesus were so convinced of the importance of this message that they devoted their lives to making it known, and almost all of them died a martyr's death because of it.[1]

But what precisely was this message? It is obviously more than a man dying on a cross who somehow was able to overcome death. What do these two events have to do with the human race and specifically with you and me? Or to put it another way, what does all this talk about crucifixion and resurrection have to do with the world in which you and I live?

Before delving into the specifics of this message, there is one fundamental realization that we have to come to grips with, and that

---

[1] See the following sources for information about the deaths of Jesus's disciples: *Foxe's Book of Martyrs* (New Kensington, PA: Whitaker House, 1981);William S. McBirnie, *The Search for the Twelve Apostles* (Carol Stream, IL: Tyndale, 2008); C. Bernard Ruffin, *The Twelve—The Lives of the Apostles after Calvary* (Huntington, IN: Our Sunday Visitor, 1997).

involves the fact that we humans are flawed both in terms of our morality and our behavior. Whether we want to admit it or not, we do not do the things we know we should, or behave as we wish we could. Very few will admit that in a public setting, but in the privacy of our own thoughts we know that we are not what we deeply desire to be. All we need to do is reflect on the activities of any given day, and if we are honest with ourselves, we know we are flawed. We characteristically fail to treat people as we ourselves desire to be treated. We say things that hurt those around us and bring shame to ourselves and those we love. Our passions often determine our behavior, and we justify this behavior by telling ourselves that we deserve the pleasure we seek. If someone gets hurt in the process, "so be it," we say. Fulfilling our selfish desires seems much more important than the adverse consequences for others from our misplaced passions. When we are alone and have time to reflect, the "high" that we experienced is long since gone and the reality of who we are "strikes home," leaving us with an emptiness that is worse than the transient happiness we thought would last. And this is in addition to the fractured relationships that result from the gratifications of our desires.

One does not need to be a criminal or sociopath to understand these realities. They are experiences with which we can all identify. "What we want to do, we find ourselves not doing, and what we don't want to do, we find ourselves doing" was the way the apostle Paul described these circumstances when reviewing his own life (see Rom. 7:15–20). And again, if we are honest, we long for deliverance from this bondage, as Paul further echoed (see Rom. 7:22–25).

The Scriptures refer to this flawed condition as our sinful nature.

"Our sinful nature!" I hear someone exclaiming. "You've got to be kidding! I thought we were beyond this 'sin' stuff. I may agree that I'm not everything I'd like to be as a human being; I will even admit that I'm imperfect, perhaps flawed, as you say, but a 'sinner'? No way! I thought this 'sin' language went out years ago. After all, don't we live in the twenty-first century?"

It might come as a surprise to someone making such comments that the word *sin* is actually a synonym for being imperfect or flawed. While commonly used as a description of doing bad things or breaking a moral code, such as the Ten Commandments, its root meaning really has to do with "not measuring up." Both the Hebrew word for sin (*het'*) in the Old Testament and the Greek word for sin (*hamartia*) in the New Testament have the same meaning, namely to "miss the mark" or "miss the target."[2] In fact, in ancient times sin was an archery term used to designate missing the target. When an archer took his bow and released his arrow with the intent of hitting the bull's-eye, if he missed the target, he had "sinned," or missed the mark.[3] It did not matter whether he missed by a sixteenth of an inch or two feet. In either case, he had still fallen short of his intended goal.

The same is true with us as sinful humans. Each of us is constantly trying to find meaning and purpose in life, but because of our flawed priorities we are continually "missing the mark." As Tim Keller has so aptly noted in his book *The Reason for God*,

> Every person must find *some* way to "justify their existence," and to stave off the universal fear that they're "a bum.". . . There are an infinite variety of identity-bases. Some get their sense of "self" from gaining and wielding power, others from human approval, others from self-discipline and control. But everyone is building their identity on something.[4]

The problem is that in attempting to find our identity and self-worth, we search in all the wrong places, failing to recognize that we were created to live in relationship with God. Recalling the nineteenth-century Danish philosopher Søren Kierkegaard, Keller further notes,

> . . . human beings were made not only to believe in God, . . . but to love him supremely, center their lives on him above everything else, and

---

[2] *Tyndale Bible Dictionary*, ed. Walter A. Elwell and Philip W. Comfort (Carol Stream, IL: Tyndale, 2001), 1203–1204.

[3] Marvin R. Wilson, *Our Father Abraham: Jewish Roots of the Christian Faith* (Grand Rapids, MI: Eerdmans, 1989), 126–127 (he discusses the linkage between the archery term for "missing the mark or target" and the biblical concept of sin).

[4] Timothy Keller, *The Reason for God* (New York: Dutton, 2008), 164. Keller has in view Kierkegaard's book *The Sickness unto Death*," originally published in 1849. For the relevant portion, see the 1989 Penguin edition, pages 111–113.

build their very identities on him. Anything other than this is sin. . . . [thus] the primary way to define sin is not just the doing of bad things, but the making of good things into *ultimate* things. It is seeking to establish a sense of self by making something else more central to your significance, purpose, and happiness than your relationship to God.[5]

As Paul said in Romans 3:23, "all have sinned [i.e., missed the mark] and fall short of the glory of God [i.e., God's perfect intentions for us]."

The implications of this sinful condition are far-reaching and encompass every dimension of our lives. As emphasized in his book *Sin and Grace*, Mark McMinn has identified *functional, structural,* and *relational* implications of our sinful nature:

> From a functional perspective, God created humans and instructed them to manage themselves and creation with goodness and self-control. We have fallen short. Wars divide our world, pollution produced for the sake of convenience and profit threatens the health of creation, and our failures of self-control are evident everywhere—in crime, addiction, poverty, pornography, violence, gluttony, consumerism and so much more.
>
> From a structural vantage point, God created humans with certain ontological capacities, to speak and reason and understand morality. These capacities have been compromised by . . . sin. . . . Because of this sinful nature, our God-given structural capacities are weakened and distorted. Our capacity to think well, to determine the moral alternative, to understand the complexities of the created order have all been tainted by our sinful nature. Our human will has become corrupted and twisted, even before we consciously chose sin, so that we do not naturally love God first and neighbor as self . . . .
>
> Here again, we see the devastating consequences of sin. Our relationships have been damaged—both our relationships with other humans and our relationship with God. Conflict is all around us, ranging from interpersonal to international, and we have turned away from God—the source of greatest joy—in our relentless quest for personal fulfillment and pleasure . . . .
>
> In all these ways we see the wreckage of sin extending through all creation.[6]

---

[5] Ibid., 162.
[6] Mark R. McMinn, *Sin and Grace in Christian Counseling: An Integrative Paradigm* (Downers Grove, IL: InterVarsity Press, 2008), 23–24.

It is at this juncture that the death of Jesus takes on a level of meaning beyond the notion that it was merely the sad end point of a plot by his enemies to silence his message. The crucifixion was not some unfortunate accident, but the masterful plan of God himself to enable you and me, and every other human being, to enter into a relationship with him. One cannot seriously read the New Testament without gleaning this resounding message from its pages. Jesus himself on multiple occasions spoke of his impending death and linked this event with the reason for his entering our world. On one occasion he said, "The Son of Man [referring to himself] is going to be delivered into the hands of men, and they will kill him. And when he is killed, after three days he will rise" (Mark 9:31). On another occasion, he referred to himself as a shepherd tending sheep (meaning people like you and me) and made this bold statement: "I am the good shepherd. The good shepherd lays down his life for the sheep. . . . For this reason the Father loves me, because I lay down my life that I may take it up again. No one takes it from me, but I lay it down of my own accord" (John 10:11–18). On yet another occasion, anticipating the agony and shame of the cross, he exclaims, "Now my soul is troubled. And what shall I say? 'Father, save me from this hour'? But for this purpose I have come to this hour" (John 12:27). Similarly, the apostle Paul states in Romans 5:6–8, ". . . Christ died for the ungodly. For one will scarcely die for a righteous person—though perhaps for a good person one would dare even to die—but God shows his love for us in that while we were still sinners, Christ died for us." Finally, the apostle Peter, when speaking of Jesus, made an equally bold assertion in his first epistle: "He committed no sin, neither was deceit found in his mouth. When he was reviled, he did not revile in return; when he suffered, he did not threaten, but continued entrusting himself to him [referring to God] who judges justly. He himself bore our sins in his body on the tree, that we might die to sin and live to righteousness. By his wounds you have been healed" (1 Pet. 2:22–24).

So what happened on the cross, and how does that impact you and me? While many theological terms can be used to answer these questions, three overarching concepts best capture the significance of the crucifixion. These concepts include forgiveness, redemption, and restoration.

As previously noted, our sinful condition has brought about a fractured relationship with the God who created us. As is true of any relationship that has been disrupted, forgiveness is an essential ingredient of its reestablishment, because somewhere in the severing of the relationship, trust has been undermined. *Forgiveness* can be defined in a number of ways, but it is basically the act of relinquishing the resentment, indignation, hate, or anger caused by an offense. The result of this action is that the demand for punishment, restitution or "payback" from the person committing the harm is no longer claimed and that individual is granted free pardon.

But there is always a cost to the person offering the forgiveness. Take, for example, the situation where a person circulates gossip about someone who had considered him a friend. Since gossip usually has an element of dishonesty associated with it and often contains information that was intended to remain confidential, the person being gossiped about can suffer considerable consequences. Not only can gossip bring shame and disrespect to that person, but depending on how believable it may sound, it can also result in serious repercussions for the victim, such as being ostracized by friends or even having one's employment compromised. The natural response is for the victim of the gossip to seek retribution against the one spreading the gossip. If, instead, the victim freely offers forgiveness, not only has he exerted all the effort to bring about the forgiveness, but he has also borne the cost of the consequences resulting from the offense. And it is indeed often the case that the victim must initiate reconciliation, either because the person responsible for the gossip is unwilling to acknowledge his egregious action or because he does not know how to reach out to the one he has harmed, to initiate healing.

In a much more magnificent and mind-boggling fashion, God has done the same thing for us in initiating our reconciliation with him. His original intent when he created us was to be in relationship with us. As such, we were to respect and honor him as our Maker, not only with our words but also with our actions. The terms of that relationship were later clearly spelled out in the Ten Commandments, which articulated how we were to relate to him as well as to our fellow humans (see Ex. 20:1–17). It does not take a genius to realize that we have fallen far short in living out these expectations. Our self-conceit and pride have dishonored God at every turn and have wreaked havoc on our relationships with others. Needless to say, we have made a mess of things. Accordingly, God has every right to distance himself from us and even to disown us. But in his amazing love, he chose not to do this and instead offers us his forgiving mercy.

This forgiveness, however, has been provided at an enormous cost. For it could happen only through the death of God's Son, Jesus, on our behalf. In his thoughtfully written book *Who Is This Jesus?* Michael Green has captured the wonder of it all:

> . . . the cross of Jesus . . . was . . . *a solution of complete fairness.* God had a problem with us. It stretched back to the first man. From the dawn of time we humans have chosen to go our own way. We have been rebels, hostile, ungrateful, and self-centered, experiencing all the human misery to which that self-centeredness leads. This is true, and we all know it. It is futile to deny it. The heart of our problems is the problem of our hearts. And what is God to do about it? He could, I suppose, force us to go His way, like a train, fated to follow the rails. But where, then, would be the free will with which alone we could respond to His love? He could, I suppose, condemn us to the permanent separation from Him that our lives deserve and that we have already chosen for ourselves. In that case there would be no hope for us. Or He could, perhaps, pretend that our sins and wicked deeds do not matter, pat us on the head, and imagine all in the garden is lovely when He knows—and we know—it is not. But God is not into a game of make-believe. Where would be His integrity, His Justice, if He did that? Where would be the difference between right and wrong? No, none of these possible solutions had any mileage in it.
>
> But in the cross of Jesus I see a solution of complete fairness: God could be totally just and fair, on the one hand, and could have people like us back into His company, on the other. What He did is breathtaking in its boldness, unassailable in its justice, and earthshaking in its generosity. He took our place! He condemned the wickedness of human beings and took the condemnation in His own person. He faced up to the poison in human hearts and drank the bitter cup of death

Himself. He did not pretend that our debts to Him were not astronomi-
cal. But He paid for them out of His own account, and it crushed Him.
Is that not the most incredible love?

Some people present it as a cold transaction, as if God the Father
punished Jesus in our place. Often they back it up with legal analogies,
which are less than just and less than helpful—as if a judge would cause
(or even allow) the wrong person to be punished. That is not God's way.
What He did was absolutely just and fair. It was the solution that gave
complete satisfaction both to His holiness and to His love. He upheld
the penalty we deserved—and then went and endured it Himself. And
because Jesus was *human,* it was a person standing for the human race
at the place of our greatest need. Because Jesus was *God* as well as man,
the effect of what He has done is limitless. It explains how God could
accept people like Abraham and David in Old Testament days who
knew nothing of Christ but were clearly reveling in divine forgiveness.
They were forgiven because of what Jesus was going to do on the cross.
It explains how God can accept us, so many centuries later, because of
what Jesus did, once and for all, on the cross. . . . As John, that close
friend of Jesus put it: [Jesus] is the expiation for our sins, and not for
ours only but also for the sins of the whole world (1 John 2:2). . . .

Sometimes when we encounter sheer generosity on a massive
scale, we feel embarrassed. But at other times our eyes light up with
wonder, and we throw ourselves into the arms of our generous bene-
factor. This is what Jesus Christ wants us to do in response to His
breathtaking gift.[7]

Not only does Jesus's death make our forgiveness possible, it also
ensures our *redemption.* While not as familiar as the word *forgiveness,* redemption is associated with several important implications for
the Christian. Its root meaning includes ideas of being released from
bondage, rescued from entrapment, or purchased back from someone
else's possession, such as buying back something that may have been
pawned. From a Christian perspective, our redemption first guarantees that sin no longer controls us. It is one thing to be forgiven of our
sin; it is quite another to be delivered from its power, as redemption
implies. Second, the penalty of sin, which is death itself, has been paid
on our behalf by Jesus's sacrificial death. We now have the hope of

---

[7] Michael Green, *Who Is This Jesus?* (Nashville: Thomas Nelson, 1992), 72–75 (I am deeply grateful to
Michael Green for permission to use this quote).

eternal life since the debt that we incurred from sin's wages (see Rom. 6:23) has been paid in full by Jesus himself. Finally, the bondage that has held us in sin's grip, so that we have been unable to become the kind of people God intended us to be, has now been severed by Jesus's redemptive power. It is as though we have been provided a means of escape from the dark dungeon that has confined and trapped us all our lives, and are now for the first time experiencing the liberating joy of freedom itself. As John's Gospel puts it, "So if the Son [referring to Jesus] sets you free, you will be free indeed" (John 8:36).

The third word of importance, in considering the significance of the crucifixion, is *restoration*. Whenever I think of this word, I am reminded of a friend who restores cars. He's been doing this for years, and it is amazing how he can take an old car that most people would call "junk" and not only refurbish it so that it looks brand-new, but also rebuild the engine so that it can tackle the challenges of driving on a modern expressway. In a similar way, but much more profoundly, God is in the restoration business. No matter how much of a mess we may have made of our lives, he wants to take that mess and totally rebuild us so that we become what he created us to be. This rebuilding process is not just about outward appearances; it includes a total renovation from within. In fact, until we are inwardly changed, any outward change is superficial and temporary. The theological word for this restorative process is "sanctification." I have always found this word cumbersome and difficult to relate to everyday life. For me at least, "restoration" conjures up more meaningful images.

So how does this restoration occur? Through the indwelling Spirit of God himself. Paul describes this transformation with the thought that, through the Spirit, we are now being "conformed to the image of his Son," Jesus (Rom. 8:29). This concept of being an image-bearer of Christ captures it all, for in so doing we have been called to think like him, behave like him, react to human need as he would react, and solve problems as he would solve them. In short, we are to love our fellow man as we in turn would wish to be loved. As wonderful as all of this may sound, however, it is impossible to achieve without God's Spirit making it happen.

These three interconnecting life-changing events—*forgiveness, redemption,* and *restoration*—are collectively referred to in Scripture as "salvation," or, when used as a verb, being "saved." Although such words are not commonly expressed in most people's everyday vocabulary, salvation literally means being rescued or delivered from harm's way (i.e., from sin and death) and being transferred to a state of safety and security (i.e., life).[8] This is why Jesus is called "Savior" throughout the New Testament. The image that comes to my mind as a surgeon is being delivered from a state of disease to one of wholeness, as when a cancerous tumor is removed or a source of infection is drained and eradicated. Thus, Jesus becomes the means by which we are made whole from our state of brokenness. Other words the New Testament uses for salvation include "new birth," "new creation," and "born again."

As wonderful as Jesus's death is on our behalf, enabling us to have a relationship with God, it is *absolutely* of no avail if the resurrection did not occur. Why? Because without a resurrection, the power of death would be greater than the power of God, indicating that he is not at all as powerful as the Scriptures claim that he is. Further, Jesus's death would be meaningless, and any promise that you and I could be forgiven of our sins and given the power to change our lives would be only hollow expectations. Finally, the hope of eternal life would be nothing more than a fairy tale, and those who have already died believing in this hope would forever remain in their lost state. As the apostle Paul so aptly stated, ". . . if Christ has not been raised, your faith is futile and you are still in your sins. Then those also who have fallen asleep in Christ have perished. If in Christ we have hope in this life only, we are of all people most to be pitied" (1 Cor. 15:17–19).

As we have seen, the resurrection of Jesus was not a "spiritual" resurrection, but one in which Jesus truly rose from the dead in bodily form. If the resurrection was only in some spiritual sense, Jesus did not overcome death and he is totally powerless to help us. While his death may have been noble and valiant, if he did not then physically

---

[8] For a helpful definition of salvation, see *Tyndale Bible Dictionary*, ed. Walter A Elwell and Philip W. Comfort (Carol Stream, IL: Tyndale, 2001), 1152–1153.

rise from the dead, his death has no value for us. Fortunately, the resurrection really did happen, in bodily form, and death really was conquered through the power of God. This being the case, Jesus truly can change us as he promised and can make us into "new creations." But how is this accomplished? It is one thing for claims to be made, but quite another to actually experience them. What has to be done to make these claims effectual?

The good news is that *nothing* needs to be done! And this truly is good news, since we humans are totally incapable of changing ourselves into the kind of people that we desperately long to become. We are already well aware that, despite our best intentions and even our best efforts to try and reform ourselves, we always fall short of the goal. And why is this so? Because the goal that we long to reach is the same goal that God desires for each of us, and until he does for us what we cannot do for ourselves, we will forever strive to achieve something that simply cannot be realized.

So how can this be good news? It is good news because the change that is required has already been provided on our behalf through Jesus's death on the cross. There is nothing we have done to merit it, and there is nothing we can do to earn it. It is purely an expression of God's graciousness to us and his love for us.

It is precisely because this salvation is a gift that it becomes a stumbling block for so many. In a competitive society such as ours, where we are expected to earn everything that is considered of value, and the concept of "free" is always under suspicion, the idea that we are being given a "gift" is commonly viewed with disbelief. And yet it is this gift, freely given by God, that sets Christianity apart from every other religion and faith tradition. Every other worldview that seeks to know God requires man to do something. This can range from keeping a set of rules and regulations, or behaving in a certain way, to practicing various rituals and ceremonies. Christianity teaches that none of these actions can bring us to God; the gulf that exists between him and us because of our sin is simply too great. Only Jesus's sacrifice on the cross can bridge that gulf and reestablish this fractured relationship.

Commenting further on this issue and the importance of Jesus's death on our behalf, John R. W. Stott offers these insights:

> Sin had separated us from God; but Christ wanted to bring us back to God. So he suffered for our sins, an innocent Savior dying for guilty sinners. And he did it just the "once," decisively, so that what he did cannot be repeated or improved upon or even supplemented.
>
> We must not miss what this implies. It means that no religious observance or good behavior on our part could ever earn our forgiveness. Yet a great many people accept the caricature of Christianity that claims that we can. They see religion as a system of human merit. "God helps those who help themselves," they say. But there is no way that this view can be reconciled with the cross of Christ. He died to take away our sins for the simple reason that we cannot remove them ourselves. If we could, his atoning death would be unnecessary. Indeed, to claim that we can end up in God's good books by our own efforts is an insult to Jesus Christ. It is equivalent to saying that we can manage without him and that he really need not have bothered to die. As Paul put it, "if righteousness (i.e., being put right with God) could be gained through the law (i.e., through us keeping the rules), Christ died for nothing!" (Gal 2:21)
>
> The message of the cross remains, in our day as in Paul's, foolishness to the wise and a stumbling block to the self-righteous, but it has brought peace to the conscience of millions. There is healing through the wounds of Christ, life through his death, pardon through his pain, salvation through his suffering.[9]

So how does this great salvation become mine personally? Through faith in this Jesus who made it all possible. Here, having *faith* means having the confidence that, by believing in Jesus's saving power, I can be rescued from my sinful condition and restored into relationship with the God who created me. As Acts 16:31 puts it, "Believe in the Lord Jesus, and you will be saved." Or to use the words of Jesus himself in John 3:16, "For God so loved the world, that he gave his only Son [referring to himself], that whoever believes in him should not perish but have eternal life."

This faith is not some blind superstition, as those who have no

---

[9] John R. W. Stott, *Basic Christianity* (1958; repr., Grand Rapids, MI: Eerdmans, 2008), 117.

place for Christianity in their worldview would have us believe, but the assurance that God will accomplish a total renovation of our lives if we simply ask him to do so. To demonstrate that faith is not some abstract concept restricted to Christian thinking, consider the relationship between a patient and a surgeon when an operation is needed. A key element in preparing for a surgical operation is that the patient must sign a permit to allow the procedure to move forward. If the permit is not signed, the operation will not occur no matter how urgent it may be. This can be a very frightening situation for the patient. He is aware that an operation must be performed, but now he is being asked to entrust his life to a person whom he may not even know. Under the best of circumstances, this patient may know something about the surgeon's training, his alleged skill in carrying out the operation in question, and his track record in that particular procedure. Sometimes the patient learns about the skills of a particular surgeon through a friend who experienced a successful outcome under his care. In most cases, however, the patient does not have this fund of knowledge and simply commits his life to a surgeon to whom he was referred by his primary care physician. In my own experience, I have tried my best to reassure the patient at the time of obtaining the permit by telling him something about my training, my experience with performing the procedure, and the results that have generally been achievable. In the end, however, the patient is totally at my mercy, with the expectation of a positive outcome. I take this trust very seriously and do everything I humanly can to ensure that the result is as anticipated. This trust that the patient puts in me is basically "faith," hopefully based not on some blind trust but on reasonable confidence. Despite my best efforts, though, the operation does not always turn out as planned, making the end result less than satisfying for both the patient and me. Fortunately, this is the exception rather than the rule.

Now return with me to the issue of exercising faith in Jesus to provide for our forgiveness from sin, redemption from its power and penalty, and restoration into a whole new dimension of living. In contrast to the uncertainties and potential risks characterizing the surgeon-patient relationship, there are no risks in entrusting our lives to the saving power of Jesus. He has already accomplished everything that needs to be done, when he died on our behalf on the cross. Everything that could keep us separated from God has been forever dealt with. And to show how trustworthy Jesus really is, he voluntarily allowed himself to die so that we might live. Further, unlike a surgical procedure, in which things are sometimes overlooked that may be needed to fully correct a problem, nothing was overlooked on the cross.

And as validation for this perfect sacrifice that Jesus offered on our behalf, God raised him from the dead. This is why the resurrection is so important. Without it, we have no way of knowing whether Jesus truly can save us. With it, all questions in this regard have been forever silenced. When we place our faith in Jesus to save us, it is not some blind confidence that we hope will turn out in our favor, but a faith based on reason. It is a faith that can be completely trusted on two counts: *first*, the total adequacy of Jesus's sacrifice; and *second*, the verification of that adequacy when Jesus conquered the final penalty of sin, even death itself, through his resurrection. As a surgeon, the guarantees I offer a patient are limited by my human frailties and by the unpredictability of situations that may come up during the surgery. As the God-man, though, there are no limitations with Jesus and no unpredictable situations that he cannot remedy. He truly is able to save us "to the uttermost," as an old Christian hymn proclaims[10] (see also Heb. 7:25).

While I fully recognize that there is mystery to this salvation that our minds will never entirely grasp, do not get sidetracked by this mystery so that you miss the liberating power that it was intended to give. Many have missed it because they have been too busy analyzing it to see if it measures up to their preconceived notions. I have been married to my wife for more than forty years, and sometimes, when I reflect on my faults, limitations, and deficiencies, I wonder why she has stayed with me for so long. The answer is because she loves me! If I sit around analyzing why, I miss out on the wonderful relationship I have been privileged to enjoy by having her as my mate. Even though

---

[10] William J. Kirkpatrick, "Saved to the Uttermost, I Am the Lord's."

there is mystery, from my perspective, as to why she would love me, I decided long ago not to get bogged down trying to explain it—and simply to enjoy it!

On a much larger scale, the God of this universe has chosen to love us and has desired to be in relationship with us. I can sit around indefinitely attempting to explain this love, but try as I may, a satisfactory answer will never be forthcoming. Only he knows fully why he chose you and me to be recipients of his love. He is not asking us to explain it, analyze it, or comprehend it, but simply to receive it. And if we will receive it he has promised forgiveness, redemption, and restoration through what his Son, Jesus, accomplished on the cross. The only thing that remains is whether you and I will accept that love gift and allow him to change us into the men and women he intended us to be. I accepted that invitation many years ago and have never regretted doing so. Hopefully, you will respond in the same way if you have not already done so.

The title of this chapter raised the question of why Jesus died. It should be obvious by now that his death was not some unfortunate historical accident but was divinely planned for our salvation. This is why the cross has been such an essential component of the Christian message for the past two thousand years. Without it, Christianity ceases to exist. But this message is meaningless rhetoric if Jesus is buried somewhere in a Middle Eastern tomb, because the liberation from sin that was intended to come from his death can only be actualized if the ultimate penalty of sin, even death itself, was forever overcome. Fortunately, Jesus is not in a tomb, and he did overcome death just as he said he would. Thus, the second component of the Christian message is Jesus's resurrection, which forever validates the saving power of his death.

These two components form the backbone of Christianity. One need only read the book of Acts and it becomes clear that the death and resurrection of Jesus were always linked in the early church, and that without the resurrection Jesus's death had no meaning. Although various attempts have been made in recent years to water down this message by presenting a Jesus who died but did not overcome death, as though this were sufficient for our salvation, nothing can be further from the truth. A dead Jesus has no saving power. The apostle Peter's first sermon is the message of Christianity and must remain so if we are to be delivered from our sins and enjoy the reality of eternal life. The essence of that message is a fitting conclusion to this chapter:

> "Men of Israel, hear these words: Jesus of Nazareth, a man attested to you by God with mighty works and wonders and signs that God did through him in your midst, as you yourselves know—this Jesus, delivered up according to the definite plan and foreknowledge of God, you crucified and killed by the hands of lawless men. God raised him up, loosing the pangs of death, because it was not possible for him to be held by it." . . .
>
> "Brothers, I may say to you with confidence about the patriarch David that he both died and was buried, and his tomb is with us to this day. Being therefore a prophet, and knowing that God had sworn with an oath to him that he would set one of his descendants on his throne, he foresaw and spoke about the resurrection of the Christ, that he was not abandoned to Hades, nor did his flesh see corruption. This Jesus God raised up, and of that we are all witnesses. . . .
>
> "Let all the house of Israel therefore know for certain that God has made him both Lord and Christ, this Jesus whom you crucified . . . .
>
> "Repent and be baptized every one of you in the name of Jesus Christ for the forgiveness of your sins, and you will receive the gift of the Holy Spirit." (Acts 2:22–24, 29–32, 36, 38)

9

EPILOGUE:
THE KEY THAT FITS THE LOCK

As I was completing the final chapters of this book, the brevity of life and the unpredictability of death were again driven home to me, this time in a very personal way. Two people who were more than just passing acquaintances died very unexpectedly. One was a relative by marriage, who along with her husband had stayed with my wife and me some two months previously, when they used our home as their base of operations (they lived in the Midwest) to visit children and grandchildren living in various parts of Virginia. We spent many hours together reconnecting, and could not have anticipated in our wildest dreams that she would be taken from us sixty days later at the age of 64, apparently of a massive heart attack. The other person was a young nurse, age 49, with whom I had worked for a number of years. This woman was the picture of excellent health, physically fit, with an attitude of positivity and compassion. The day before her death of a massive stroke, I had spent two hours with her and several other colleagues brainstorming how to make our operating rooms more efficient. Little could I have known that this would be the last time I would see her alive.

So what happened to these two people? Do they now cease to exist, or have they entered into a new sphere of afterlife? If one sees life through the lens of a materialistic, naturalistic worldview and believes that humans are nothing more than the most highly evolved members of the animal kingdom, then the absence of any further existence after death is the only rational answer. This view proposes that, when our bodies cease to function, we simply cease to exist. Many in the scientific community espouse this worldview, Dawkins and Provine among them as previously noted.[1]

But are humans simply collections of cells that, once dead, undergo annihilation, or is there another dimension of being alive that cannot be defined in solely materialistic terms? Christianity proposes that man was created to be in relationship with God, and that Jesus entered our world to make that happen. It makes no sense, then, to think that such a relationship would cease at the time of one's death, with no eternal implications. The whole purpose of Jesus's death was to make possible the restoration of the relationship with our Creator that had been severed by our sinful condition. To think that his death had meaning only for the short time that we humans enjoy life on Planet Earth goes against the whole Christian message that we were intended to live forever. Further, the resurrection of Jesus is the validating event that affirms once and for all that Jesus's sacrifice was acceptable to God and nothing more needed to be done to bring us into relationship with him.

Returning to the deaths of these two women, Christianity has much to say about their current state. Taking John 3:16 at face value, both women had expressed faith in the saving work of Jesus to restore their fractured relationship with the God who created them. If this verse can be trusted, as the resurrection of Jesus guarantees that it can be, then not only are they at this moment very much alive, but their new life will continue forever. While it is not my intent to get into an exhaustive discussion of the "afterlife," an important thesis of Christianity is that we humans are more than just a compilation of material cells; we also have a soul/spirit component, having been created in God's image.[2] For the believer in Jesus, this soul/spirit component goes to be with Jesus at the time of death. The apostle Paul

---

[1] Richard Dawkins, *The God Delusion* (New York: Houghton Mifflin, 2006); William B. Provine, in "Darwinism: Science or Naturalistic Philosophy" (debate between William B. Provine and Phillip E. Johnson at Stanford University, April 30, 1994; published in *Origins Research* 16/1 [Fall/Winter 1994]: 9).

[2] Two excellent books on what the Bible has to say regarding life beyond the grave are Anthony A. Hoekema, *The Bible and the Future* (Grand Rapids, MI: Eerdmans, 1979); Randy Alcorn, *Heaven* (Carol Stream, IL: Tyndale, 2004).

captured this transition in the phrase "away from the body and at home with the Lord" (2 Cor. 5:8). At some future date Jesus will come a second time to establish his eternal kingdom (the first time being his entrance into our world some twenty centuries ago). When he comes again, the deceased bodies of believers will be resurrected from the dead to be reunited with their soul/spirits. Paul speaks of this event in 1 Thessalonians 4:13–18:

> . . . we do not want you to be uninformed, brothers, about those who are asleep, that you may not grieve as others do who have no hope. For since we believe that Jesus died and rose again, even so, through Jesus, God will bring with him those who have fallen asleep. For this we declare to you by a word from the Lord, that we who are alive, who are left until the coming of the Lord, will not precede those who have fallen asleep. For the Lord himself will descend from heaven with a cry of command, with the voice of an archangel, and with the sound of the trumpet of God. And the dead in Christ will rise first. Then we who are alive, who are left, will be caught up together with them in the clouds to meet the Lord in the air, and so we will always be with the Lord. Therefore encourage one another with these words.

The blissfulness of this heavenly state is further described in Revelation, the final book of the Bible:

> Then I saw a new heaven and a new earth, for the first heaven and the first earth had passed away, and the sea was no more. And I saw the holy city, new Jerusalem, coming down out of heaven from God, prepared as a bride adorned for her husband. And I heard a loud voice from the throne saying, "Behold, the dwelling place of God is with man. He will dwell with them, and they will be his people, and God himself will be with them as their God. He will wipe away every tear from their eyes, and death shall be no more, neither shall there be mourning, nor crying, nor pain anymore, for the former things have passed away." (Rev. 21:1–4)

This magnificent future for the believer in Jesus is totally a hoax, though, if the resurrection did not occur. As Paul explains,

> . . . if Christ has not been raised, your faith is futile and you are still in your sins. Then those also who have fallen asleep in Christ have

perished. If in Christ we have hope in this life only, we are of all people most to be pitied. (1 Cor. 15:17–19)

Thankfully, Jesus's resurrection has occurred, so that there is a glorious hope not only for the two women just discussed, but for every other believer as well who has trusted Jesus as Lord and Savior. Whether we are dead or alive when Jesus returns, Christianity maintains that our bodies will instantaneously change to be like his resurrection body, never to be subject to death again. The apostle Paul, once more, captures the incredible implications of this event:

> Behold! I tell you a mystery. We shall not all sleep, but we shall all be changed, in a moment, in the twinkling of an eye, at the last trumpet. For the trumpet will sound, and the dead will be raised [i.e., resurrected] imperishable, and we shall be changed. For this perishable body must put on the imperishable, and this mortal body must put on immortality. When the perishable puts on the imperishable, and the mortal puts on immortality, then shall come to pass the saying that is written:
>
> > "Death is swallowed up in victory."
> > "O death, where is your victory?
> > O death, where is your sting?"
>
> The sting of death is sin, and the power of sin is the law. But thanks be to God, who gives us the victory through our Lord Jesus Christ. (1 Cor. 15:51–57)

Despite the indescribable future that the Scriptures assert awaits the believer in Jesus, there are surely those reading this book who would challenge these biblical proclamations. For such people, the resurrection is nothing more than a myth, and any chance of life beyond the grave is rubbish. You may be among this group. While, for me, the evidence we have considered overwhelmingly supports the conclusion that Jesus truly died by crucifixion and several days later rose from the dead in a real, three-dimensional body, it is certainly your prerogative to evaluate this evidence and conclude differently. I only request that you deal with the evidence fairly and honestly and offer cogent reasons for rejecting it. It is not good enough to simply ignore the evidence, trash it, or refuse to grapple with it because it goes against preconceived notions. The common objection that miracles such as the resurrection simply do not occur, and thus "case closed," is not acceptable. How do you know that miracles do not occur? On what basis have you reached that conclusion? And how do you determine what is and what is not truth? And if there is a God, how do you know that he does not occasionally invade the orderliness of his universe by doing something different and unexplainable? Couldn't the resurrection be an example of this? And even if you do not believe there is a God, does that guarantee that he does not exist? In short, the evidence presented in this book for the resurrection of Jesus shouts for acceptance. The burden of proof is on you to disprove it.

If, like me, you are convinced that Jesus truly did conquer death, then it is important that you not stop there and simply consider the resurrection an interesting historical phenomenon. For if the resurrection really happened in our space-time world, it is unlike any event that has ever occurred. Who is this man called Jesus, who was able to overcome our greatest enemy? Is there something about him that sets him apart from every other human being who ever lived? I can think of no better way to get acquainted with him than to carefully and seriously read the four Gospel accounts detailing what he was like when he lived among us. I have done that, and have never been the same since.

I am also very much aware that there may be some reading this book who come from other faith traditions or religious persuasions and are just as committed to their worldview as I am to mine. You may be one of those people. I realize that to you Jesus has been, at most, simply another religious leader, even if a good one. It is quite right and appropriate then to ask the probing question "Why should I follow Jesus if I am perfectly happy with the religion I have embraced?" This is certainly a legitimate question and one that demands an answer. In responding to it, I would ask two further questions: "What can you tell me about the founder of your religion?" and, "Does your religion adequately address the needs of your life?"

Concerning the first question, it is important to know whether the founder of your religion is dead or alive. If your religion has been around for hundreds or perhaps thousands of years, I would suspect that he is dead and that the site of his burial is known and is regarded as sacred to his followers. This person may also have been a great teacher, and many of his teachings may be available to us in some sacred book. Not for an instant would I demean this person. But the very fact that he is dead tells me that he is not eternal or supernatural. On that count alone, he does not measure up to the person who is celebrated and worshiped in Christianity. If you contend that your spiritual leader is alive and has conquered death, what is your evidence? I have presented my evidence on behalf of Jesus. What is yours?

Regarding the adequacy of your religion to meet the needs of your life, how relevant to your personal life situation is it? Does it only have relevance on some "holy day," or does it have meaning each day of your life? How does it answer the ultimate questions we humans struggle with, such as, Who am I? Why am I here? Where am I going when I die? Consider a puzzle made up of a hundred pieces, each of which when interlocked with its surrounding pieces ultimately depicts a breathtaking panoramic view of the Rocky Mountains. If one focuses only on the individual pieces in isolation, with no attempt to bring them together and see their interrelatedness, these random components of the puzzle can appear meaningless, insignificant, and chaotic. It is only when they are linked together that the cohesiveness and beauty of the hidden landscape is revealed. Such is the lack of cohesiveness of most religions and philosophies, perhaps even yours. In contrast, Christianity pulls everything together and provides purpose and meaning as well as value to what otherwise would appear disjointed, futile, and hopeless.

G. K. Chesterton, whom we met earlier, spent much of his literary career defending Christianity because he thought it was the only worldview that adequately and accurately assessed the human condition and presented a sufficient remedy to redeem it. In his book *The*

Everlasting Man he went to great lengths to show that Jesus was that remedy. Toward the end of the book he uses the phrase "the key that fits the lock" to show why Christianity made sense and, in his view, was true. As he explains,

> . . . in answer to the historical query of why it [the Christian faith] was accepted and is accepted, I answer for millions of others in my reply; because it [the key] fits the lock; because it is like life. It is one among many stories; only it happens to be a true story. It is one among many philosophies; only it happens to be the truth. We accept it; and the ground is solid under our feet and the road is open before us. It does not imprison us in a dream of destiny or a consciousness of the universal delusion. It opens to us not only incredible heavens, but what seems to some an equally incredible earth, and makes it credible. This is the sort of truth that is hard to explain because it is a fact; but it is a fact to which we can call witnesses. We are Christians . . . not because we worship a key, but because we have passed a door; and felt the wind that is the trumpet of liberty blow over the land of the living.[3]

Like Chesterton, I embrace Christianity because "it fits"! Think with me for a moment, precisely how Christianity fits. It fits because it accurately defines who I am, namely a flawed human being with a sinful nature who is more interested in serving myself than the God who created me. It fits because it clearly states that no matter how diligent I may be and how hard I may try, I fall short of overcoming this sinful condition and becoming the person I would like to be. And then it fits because it tells me that I need to be rescued from this plight if I ever hope to become the person I want to be. Since all humans are in the same fix, there is no way that I can be rescued unless God does it for me. Thus, Christianity fits because it tells me that God has done exactly that, meaning that he has rescued me from my plight through his son, Jesus. It further fits because Jesus is the perfect person to orchestrate that rescue, since he is both God and man. As man, he personally knows and understands the plight I am stuck with, but as God he has the power to deliver me from it. The Christian gospel also fits because Jesus, as the perfect man, was able to pay the penalty for my

---

[3] G. K. Chesterton, *The Everlasting Man* (1925; repr., San Francisco: Ignatius, 1993), 248–249.

sins—a penalty I otherwise would have had to pay myself—through his substitutionary death on the cross, making it possible for me to be forgiven and restored into an everlasting relationship with God. Finally, Christianity fits because Jesus's resurrection has validated what he has done on my behalf. It has sealed once and for all the gift of eternal life that God has offered me through Jesus. I am unaware of any other religion or faith tradition that can deliver me from my sinful plight without asking me to do it myself—which I know full well I cannot do.

What can we conclude from these observations? It seems to me that only two options are possible. Either Christianity's close "fit" with the realities of the human condition is pure happenstance, or God orchestrated this "key that fits the lock" to rescue mankind from its sinful condition, thereby making Christianity true. You will have to decide which of these options makes the most sense. For me the close correspondence of the Christian worldview with reality is too compelling for it to be nothing more than coincidence. As such, I believe that this close fit can be explained only by acknowledging that Christianity is true. This conclusion is not unique to me, of course, since billions of people down through the centuries have also embraced Christianity, many giving their lives in its defense. Not only have these people found deliverance from sin by the Christ of Christianity, but they have also experienced "new life" to become the persons they were intended to be when God created them. That new life is available to you as well, simply for the choosing.

I bring this book to a close with the story of a Nobel laureate. His name is Richard Smalley, and he was awarded the Nobel Prize in chemistry in 1996. His work made the field of nanotechnology possible. For those unfamiliar with this term, it is the science and technology of manipulating and manufacturing materials on an atomic or molecular scale so that they can be used to devise microcomputers, deliver drugs and medications, develop micro robots, and influence a variety of other novel systems.

Dr. Smalley grew up in the Midwest as part of a very loving and supportive family who early on encouraged his interest in science. On the advice of a close relative, he commenced his undergraduate education at Hope College, a Christian liberal arts school in Holland, Michigan. Although he was exposed to a Christian worldview while there, he later admitted that spiritual things were not a high priority to him at that time in his life. After two years at Hope he transferred to the University of Michigan, where he completed an undergraduate degree, and subsequently obtained his PhD at Princeton University. His postdoctoral work was completed at the University of Chicago, following which he began his academic career at Rice University in Houston and remained there for the rest of his life. It was at Rice that he created the Center for Nanoscience and Technology, which to this day is one of the leading institutions for nanotechnology research in the world.[4]

In 1999, at age 56, he was diagnosed with non-Hodgkin's lymphoma, which later became chronic lymphocytic leukemia. Being indifferent to religion most of his life and not convinced that it was of any serious value, it was during this time that he reconsidered who Jesus was and reassessed the Christian worldview. As a result of such reevaluation, he ultimately became a Christian. During the last year of his life, in May 2005, he was presented the Hope College Distinguished Alumni Award. He was unable to receive the award in person because of his declining health. To express his gratitude to the college for choosing him, he sent a letter to the school to be read at the Alumni Weekend Awards Banquet. A portion of that letter follows:

> Hello from Texas;
>
> As I write I am at M. D. Anderson Cancer Center a few miles from my home in Houston Texas. . . .
>
> My short two years at Hope starting as a freshman in 1961 were immensely important to me. I went to chapel, studied religion and attended church more than I ever had done before, and was with people who took to these issues seriously. I valued that greatly back then. Recently I have gone back to church regularly with a new focus to understand as best I can what it is that makes Christianity so vital

---

[4]Extensive information about the life and contributions of Professor Richard Smalley can be obtained from the website of the Richard E. Smalley Institute for Nanoscale Science and Technology, at Rice University.

and powerful in the lives of billions of people today even though almost 2000 years have passed since the death and resurrection of Christ.

Although I suspect I will never fully understand, I now think the answer is very simple: It's true. God did create the universe about 13.7 billion years ago, and of necessity has involved Himself with His creation ever since. The purpose of this universe is something that only God knows for sure, but it is increasingly clear to modern science that the universe was exquisitely fine-tuned to enable human life. We are somehow critically involved in His purpose. Our job is to sense that purpose as best we can, love one another, and help Him get that job done.

I wish I could be with you tonight. Thank you for the honor of the Distinguished Alumni Award. For all of us who have had the privilege of attending this great college, we know what it means to say "Hope is my Anchor."[5]

Dr. Smalley died some five months later, on October 28, 2005. Despite being one of the most distinguished scientists of his era, he did not find being a Christian to be in conflict with his scientific pursuits. Why? Because, like many others before him, he found that "Christianity is true!"

Jesus made two bold statements during his earthly ministry that are worthy of note as we close. On one occasion he said, "you will know the truth, and the truth will set you free" (John 8:32). On another occasion he exclaimed, "I am the truth" (John 14:6).

What truth are you following? Has it set you free?

---

[5] Remarks by Richard Smalley read at 2005 Alumni Weekend Awards Banquet (posted October 29, 2005), Hope College, Office of Public Relations, 141 E. 12th St., Holland, MI 49423 [prelations@hope.edu] (used with permission of Hope College).

GENERAL INDEX

SCRIPTURE INDEX